Fire in
Thy Mouth

DONALD G. MILLER

Fire in Thy Mouth

"Behold, I will make my words
in thy mouth fire."
—Jer. 5:14

ABINGDON PRESS
New York • Nashville

FIRE IN THY MOUTH

Copyright MCMLIV by Pierce & Washabaugh

Library of Congress Catalog Card Number: 54-5229

B

SET UP, PRINTED, AND BOUND BY THE
PARTHENON PRESS, AT NASHVILLE,
TENNESSEE, UNITED STATES OF AMERICA

To

HARRIS ELLIOTT KIRK

*who for more than half a century
has made his pulpit a throne
of power at the heart of
a great city*

Preface

=◦∽◦=

THE "rediscovery" of the Bible as the source book of theology has not gone far enough—it has not reached the pulpit. Brilliant exceptions may here and there be witnessed, but they merely serve to point up the lack of a biblical basis in the average contemporary sermon.

When this question is raised among ministers, some plead guilty with unabashed boldness. For them the Bible is too dated to have much relevance to our time. Others plead not guilty. Preach from the Bible? Of course. They take a text every Sunday morning! But by various means—spiritualization, subjectivism, questionable analogy, downright misinterpretation, immediate departure from the text to the realm of their own thought—the true meaning of the text is lost.

The reasons for this neglect of the Bible in the pulpit are manifold. Lack of time for study is perhaps foremost. Most ministers are average mortals—not men of genius. Another reason is that it takes much more effort to dig out what a passage of Scripture means, and then to set that meaning in a form which can be grasped by the contemporary mind, than it does to produce other types of sermons. Another is the increasing dependence of the modern minister on homiletical helps of one sort or another. The intolerable demands of a modern parish form the occasion, and the endless flow of homiletic aids the means, by which a harassed minister finds it more and more easy to use crutches than to stretch his own intellectual muscles.

This book has been written to voice the deep conviction that there can be no true or permanent spiritual recovery until the Bible gets back into a position of centrality in the modern pulpit. However effective the various mass efforts at revivalism may be on both sides of the Atlantic, they cannot take the place of the steady impact of spiritual realities for which the local congregation is the medium. A regular diet of biblical faith is necessary to grow robust souls. The issues raised here, therefore, are not of mere academic interest. They are fundamental to the church's witness in our time. They are a passion and a plea!

Chapter I is basic to the entire argument. It is an effort to set forth a conception of preaching which is formulated from the Bible itself; that preaching is not saying words but accomplishing a Deed—the actualization of redemption in the lives of men as the redeeming word is announced and responded to in faith. This conception is the keystone on which all the rest of the argument rests. If it be true, then Chapter II follows naturally with the conviction that the Bible, as the record of God's redemptive Deed, is the only valid, basic source from which true preaching may be attempted. But to approach the Bible for sermons raises the question of the difficulty of interpreting it, which forms the heart of Chapter III. The fourth chapter sketches some values of biblical preaching which are quite likely to be absent in other types of preaching. Certain implications of the central conviction of the book in relation to the total sweep of the church's life are stated in the final chapter.

8

The central core of materials in the book was given as the Westervelt lectures on preaching at the Austin Presbyterian Theological Seminary in Austin, Texas, in February, 1951. I wish to express again my gratitude to the faculty and trustees of the seminary for the invitation to deliver the lectures and for their gracious hospitality while I was their guest. Chapter I, in slightly different form, has appeared in *Interpretation,* and much of Chapter III was published in *The Princeton Seminary Bulletin.* These journals are to be thanked for their kindness in permitting the reissuing of these materials in this book.

DONALD G. MILLER

Contents

=⊶=

11

CHAPTER I

Biblical Preaching as Redemptive Event

THE discrediting of preaching is one of the marks of our time. "Don't preach at me!" is an expression which suggests that by many preaching is held in contempt. *Webster's New International Dictionary* even gives as a definition of preaching, "To discourse in the manner of a preacher;—now usually with implication of officiousness or tediousness." A former college president writes, "A good moving picture has far more influence than a good sermon." An outstanding author—famous for his ability to interpret the spiritual values of commonplace things—after a passage on "the deft and beautiful ways in which God works," adds: "I don't think this is preaching: I hope not."

The extent, however, to which this rather low opinion of preaching has permeated the mood of our time is to be seen in the appraisal of its worth by ministers. It may not be surprising that in a day when men are inclined to sit lightly toward the claims of the gospel, they should question the value of proclaiming it. But when those who have entered the Christian ministry begin to discredit preaching, it is passing strange. Yet such is the case.

During World War II Miss Maude Royden, the noted British preacher, gave unconscious testimony to this in an article addressed to Americans: "We are being sacrificed with the rest of Europe and much of Asia on the cross of war. Think of us, if you must, as no better than the thief on the cross, but do not forget that Christ did not preach to men on the cross. Do not preach to us. Pray for us if you can. If you cannot, let us alone." [1] Apart from the fact that I should judge Christ's word to the thief on the cross—"today you will be with me in Paradise"—as good preaching, Miss Royden's war-anguished statement unconsciously discredits preaching as lofty moralizing over the state of people whose deep tragedies have never touched the life of the preacher. A more deliberate appraisal of the secondary value of preaching in the work of a minister is to be seen in a letter of a ministerial candidate: "I consider preaching as a necessary evil. I shall do as much of it as my position demands in order to qualify for the other more important tasks on which my heart is set. But I could well wish to avoid preaching almost entirely."

For every conscious or unconscious avowal of the questionable merit of preaching, however, there are a thousand silent testimonies to it in the way countless ministers relegate their pulpit work to a secondary role. It is impossible, they say, to be preacher, pastor, counselor, educator, administrator, community servant, and denominational chore boy all in one. To this it would seem that any balanced mind would assent. The point I make here, however, is this: under the necessity of making a choice of the relative importance of the various functions of the modern ministry, few are the ministers who rate their preaching at or near the top. If something must come in for meager attention, let it be the preaching. Recently more than two hundred ministers replied to a questionnaire concerning the possibility of a more

[1] "What Should a Briton Do?" *The Christian Century,* April 16, 1941, p. 523.

14

effective ministry among the industrial workers of our day. Only one of these men so much as mentioned "better preaching" as a tool of increased effectiveness.

Oppressed all week with a multitude of harassing details, there is little time left to the modern minister for sermon preparation. Sundays come in their ever-recurring seven-day cycle. And Thursday morning or—perish the thought—even Saturday afternoon comes with equal regularity to face the busy minister with the question: What shall I preach this week? There is little time to ponder. The specter of Sunday morning approaches rapidly. Perhaps a sermon starter would be a good thing! What might set the wheels turning in the preacher's mind with the swift ease of a homiletic self-starter, and set him in full motion without the normal time necessary to gain momentum? James Stewart is a good one! And for variety, although his works are a bit old now, Alexander Maclaren is a big help! And that latest book *The World's Best Sermon Illustrations,* well indexed both by subject matter and text, is indispensable.

Is this caricature? I was a parish minister for several years, and know the temptation. And if you want further evidence, there come frequently to the desks of all of us advertisements of a year's supply of sermon outlines and illustrations—for both morning and evening services—with prayer meeting talks, and a "ringer" for a youth rally thrown in as a bonus, for the tidy sum of $1.75. On the assumption that in any business sales are necessary in order to keep going, somebody must be sending the $1.75!

What is the cure for this? There is only one cure radical enough to be permanent, and that is a true understanding of what preaching is. We have a low appraisal of preaching only to the extent that we fail to grasp its significance. If we will once get a firm hold on what our job is when we stand before a congregation to preach, then never again will preaching take a secondary place in our ministry. "It is not right," said the apostles, "that we should give up preaching the word of God to serve tables" (Acts 6:2).

The Nature of Preaching

What is preaching? As Percy Ainsworth once said of something else, "I won't define it, because I want you to understand it!" We are not after a new definition of it so much as a new understanding of it. When you preach, are you doing what people think you are when they say afterward, "I enjoyed your little talk"? Or is preaching what H. H. Farmer described in *The Servant of the Word* as that which gives people "feelings of an expansive and pleasant kind," so that they "have found the hour in church enjoyable, . . . the music . . . good, the singing hearty, the decorations no offence to the eye, the curtains the right shade, the building beautiful," and have come away "feeling" better? [2]

One of the most vivid statements I have ever read of what many people think good preaching to be—and is not—is contained in a letter written by Henry Scott Holland about a sermon of Benjamin Jowett's preached in Oxford:

[Jowett] preached yesterday in Chapel amidst intense excitement. . . . He looked so fatherly and beautiful and brought out the best bell-like silvern voice with quite rich tones that he had hitherto hidden in the depth of his stomach, and preached the most lovely little practical sermon in a quite perfect style with the most wonderful grace. It was just Platonism flavoured with a little Christian charity.

It was only "an attempt to take some useful moral hints from just what happens to strike [him] in a very good, 'perhaps I

[2] (New York: Charles Scribner's Sons, 1942), p. 79. Used by permission of the publishers.

16

may be excused in saying' a Divine life." Is that preaching?
No wonder he added, "Christianity is gutted by him." [3]

What is preaching? I am indebted to P. T. Forsyth for
making articulate for me my own conception of the nature
of preaching, which I felt long before I read Forsyth but
could not quite phrase. "The Gospel is an act of God," said
Forsyth. "Its preaching must therefore be an act, a 'function'
of the great act. A true sermon is a real deed." [4] To preach
the gospel, then, is not merely to say words but to effect a
deed. To preach is not merely to stand in a pulpit and speak,
no matter how eloquently and effectively, nor even to set
forth a theology, no matter how clearly it is stated nor how
worthy the theology. To preach is to become a part of a
dynamic event wherein the living, redeeming God repro-
duces his act of redemption in a living encounter with men
through the preacher. True preaching is an extension of the
Incarnation into the contemporary moment, the transfigur-
ing of the Cross and the Resurrection from ancient facts of
a remote past into living realities of the present. A sermon
is an act wherein the crucified, risen Lord personally confronts men either to save or to judge them. Ruskin's famous
saying that a sermon is "thirty minutes to raise the dead"
was not far wide of the mark. Preachers cannot raise the
dead; only the living Christ can do that. In a real sermon,
then, Christ is the Preacher. The Preacher speaks through
the preacher.

If this be so, then much that passes for preaching among
us is not of the essence of preaching at all. Eloquence, literary
finesse, logical arrangement, sustained progression, the personal appeal of the minister, handsome appearance, intel-

[3] *Henry Scott Holland: Memoirs and Letters,* ed. Stephen Paget (New
York: E. P. Dutton and Company, 1921), pp. 33-34.
[4] *Positive Preaching and the Modern Mind* (New York: Eaton and Mains,
1907), p. 22.

17

lectual brilliance, profundity of thought, the ability to sway an audience by the subtle arts of speech—these are but the accidents, not the essence, of preaching. One could have all these and yet not preach. On the other hand, one could lack all these and yet preach. These are not to be discounted in their usefulness, for presumably a man who is richly endowed in the accidents of preaching will be more effective, if he has also the essence of it, than one who is poorly endowed. But an authentic word from God through a poor human agent is true preaching, whereas a sermon which does no more than communicate human ideas is not true preaching at all. To introduce men to God so that he and they have dealings with each other is an event of abiding eternal value, no matter how crude the introduction. On the other hand, merely to talk about God without his being present is spiritually worthless, no matter how eloquent or enjoyable the speech. No man has really preached until the two-sided encounter between him and his congregation has given way to a three-sided encounter, where God himself becomes one of the living parties to it. Ideal preaching would go even one step further, where the presence of God becomes so real that the preacher himself drops almost entirely out of the consciousness of the worshipers, so that even as the preacher speaks, they and God seem to be left alone.

Phillips Brooks tells of participating as a worshiper in just such an experience:

The minstrel who sings before you to show his skill, will be praised for his wit, and rhymes, and voice. But the courier who hurries in, breathless, to bring you a message, will be forgotten in the message that he brings. Among the many sermons I have heard, I always remember one, for the wonderful way in which it was pervaded by this quality. It was a sermon by Mr. George Macdonald, the English author, . . . and it had many of the good and bad characteristics of his interesting style. It had his brave and manly honesty, and his tendency to sentimentality. But over and through it all it had this quality: it was a message from God to these people by him. . . . As I listened, I seemed to see how weak in contrast was the way in which other preachers had amused me and challenged my admiration for the working of their minds. Here was a gospel. Here were real tidings. And you listened and forgot the preacher.[5]

It was thus that Paul described his own preaching. "We are now Christ's ambassadors," he wrote to the Corinthians, *"as though God were appealing direct to you through us"* (II Cor. 5:20, Phillips; italics mine). The function of the preacher is to announce to men amazing news so much greater than he is that men shall lose sight of the preacher in the news. What is the news? "God himself is with us!" The redeeming God is actively present, judging and redeeming now in the solemn realities of this moment. Then God really becomes the Preacher. The sermon is no longer the effort of a man to speak moving words; it has become the Deed of God. True preaching is the re-enactment of the Deed of redemption as both the atoning love and resurrection power of Christ express themselves once more through his Body, the Church.

Of this, C. H. Dodd writes:

The personality of Christ receives, so to speak, an extension in the life of His body on earth. Those "saving facts," the death and resurrection of Christ, are not merely particular facts of past history, however decisive in their effect; they are re-enacted in the experience of the Church. If Christ died to this world, so have the members of His body; if He has risen into newness of life, so have they; if He being risen from the dead, dieth no more,

[5] *Lectures on Preaching* (New York: E. P. Dutton & Co., 1877), pp. 15-16.

neither do they; if God has glorified Him, He has also glorified them.[6]

Preaching is the act through which these "saving facts" are re-enacted in the experience of the church now. A sermon, therefore, is not primarily something said, but something done. Not mere words, but a deed.

This conception of preaching flows from the very nature of the redemptive action of God in history. In the Bible, God never becomes an object of contemplation, set apart from the human scene, to be looked at, defined, described, contemplated. Rather he is always Subject, acting and reacting upon men in living relations in the ongoing drama of history. It is at this point that the Hebrew and Greek modes of thought differ radically.

Take, for example, the questions of the omniscience, the omnipresence, and the omnipotence of God. Following Greek patterns of thought, each of these doctrines could be reached as the conclusion to a syllogism. God is the Absolute. The Absolute, by its very nature as absolute, is without limitation. Since, therefore, God is the Absolute, and the Absolute can have no limitations, there can be nothing that God does not know, no place where he is not, no power beyond his own. Therefore, God is omniscient, omnipresent, and omnipotent.

Contrast with that the 139th Psalm! The psalmist is not reasoning to conclusions from premises, but stating the facts of his experience. God had confronted him, and he could not escape. Unworthy thoughts could be hidden from man's knowledge, and clever words could deceive the human apprehension, but God, the living God, knew his inmost thoughts and saw through his words even before he spoke

[6] *The Apostolic Preaching and Its Developments* (London: Hodder & Stoughton, 1944), pp. 62-63.

them. The psalmist had sinned and had tried to escape from the withering eye of God. But where could he go where God was not? Heaven? Sheol? The uttermost parts of the sea? Hide in the darkness? He could escape God nowhere, not because God was theoretically the Absolute, but because everywhere the psalmist turned he was confronted by him! The psalmist's whole life was held in the hand of the mighty God, who had created him and the universe and who was the moral Ruler who would "slay the wicked." Omniscience, omnipresence, omnipotence—they are here, but not at the end of a syllogism. They are rather facets of the character of the living God, who stood astride the pathway of the psalmist's life and beset him "behind and before." God was not an abstraction, an idea, but a living Being who met him in the solid events of daily life.

The fountain from which this awareness of the living God sprang among the Hebrews was the one unforgettable fact in their history—the Exodus. There God's wisdom, presence, and power had been manifested in a mighty deliverance, a mighty redemptive and creative act whereby the Hebrews had been brought into being as a people and launched on the stream of history. God's revelation of himself, then, initially was not in the realm of idea but in the realm of event. God told them who he was by *acting* in their behalf. Revelation always begins in God's giving of himself to men in redemptive deeds.

But the nation which the redemptive Deed brought into being was a part of the Deed itself, and the prophets who later brought the life of the nation under the scrutiny of the character of the God who had acted so mightily at the Exodus were likewise parts of the Deed. The Deed initiated at the Exodus is not to be comprehended in the moment of its instigation alone, but is to be understood only in the light

21

of what flowed from it. The initial deliverance carried within it the seed of a mightier deliverance. Because of what God had done through Moses, men looked for a greater than Moses. Because of the deliverance from the bondage of slavery in Egypt, they looked for a greater deliverance from the bondage of slavery to evil. The entire history of the people and the prophetic movement within it were a part of the action of God in history initiated at the Exodus.

Prophetic and Apostolic Preaching

When, therefore, the prophets announced the word of God to men, they were not merely making speeches or just trading with ideas about God. Their word was rather an extension into history of the redemptive Deed of God at the Exodus. Their preaching was an embodiment of the agony of redemption, initiated at the Exodus but straining to be brought to fulfillment in a yet greater deliverance. The word of the prophet was nothing other than the birth pangs of the living God, striving to bring forth "new heavens and a new earth, wherein dwelleth righteousness" (K.J.V.).

This view is confirmed by the First Epistle of Peter, when he says that the prophets

tried hard to discover to what time and to what sort of circumstances the Spirit of Christ working in them was referring. For He foretold the sufferings of Christ and the glories that should follow them. It was then made clear to them that they were dealing with matters not meant for themselves, but for you. It is these very matters which have been made plain to you by those who preached the Gospel to you by the same Spirit sent from Heaven—and these are facts to command the interest of the very angels! (I Pet. 1:11-12, Phillips).

The preaching of the prophets was none other than the Spirit of Christ *working in them*. Furthermore, their preaching was a part of the total Deed of redemption, an activity of God, who through suffering was to bring to birth a glorious order, an order which is now made available to men through the life, death, resurrection, and exaltation of Jesus Christ. Through all of their work, then, God was not an object of contemplation but the Subject who was at work through them accomplishing his purpose in the history of the world. Their words were a part of the *Deed* of redemption. They were not mere purveyors of pious ideas wrought out by the ingenuity of the human mind, nor moral observers of the contemporary scene offering ethical advice on how to be happy; but they were witnesses to what God had done, was doing, and would yet do in history for the redemption of the world. And their very preaching became a part of the divine redemptive activity.

But this dynamic quality of revelation as the actual self-giving of God in history and the relation of preaching to it as an integral part of God's saving action in history, are to be seen even more clearly in the New Testament. The heart of the New Testament is a series of events, climaxed in the great Event, the Resurrection.

The preaching of the New Testament, therefore, is nothing other than the bearing witness to this series of events. But these events are not thought of in the New Testament merely as past events, but as parts of the total Event of redemption, which spans the entire sweep of history from Creation to the Parousia. The "good news" is not plural, but singular, *euangelion.* Calvin caught this when he translated it "good and joyful message." [7] The message is of one thing— the redemptive activity of God, to which Cullmann and others refer as the "Christ-Event" or the "Christ-Deed."

[7] Cf. Paul T. Fuhrmann, "Calvin, The Expositor of Scripture," *Interpretation,* April, 1952, p. 198, footnote 59.

The Old Testament is all an integral part of the Christ-Event as preparation. The New Testament is a part of the Christ-Event as realization. The coming Parousia will climax the whole Event as consummation. The whole Event is one, from Creation to Parousia. At present it is a realized Event, but not a completed Event, just as a human life is a realized affair at the moment personal awareness develops, but is not completed until death. The witness of the New Testament preachers to the events of the birth, life, death, resurrection, and exaltation of Jesus, then, sets these parts of the redemptive movement in their relation to the whole movement, and as such the witness itself became a part of the grand redemptive Deed. So as the words of the early apostles became a part of the Deed of redemption, the very nature of revelation as redemptive action was expressing itself. Revelation is primarily something done for men. To preach is so to bear witness to that which is done *for* men that it is actually done *in* men. Preaching is a part of the *doing* of it. As a recent Swedish scholar has said: "For the early Christian and Israelite comprehension 'Word' and 'Deed' are not distinguishable. The Word is identical with the soul of the speaker. When the Word of the Lord comes to someone, so it is . . . as when the Spirit of the Lord or the Lord himself comes." [8] True preaching, then, is not achieved until the words of the preacher become the Deed of God. The ultimate question for the preacher is not, "Has my sermon *said* something?" but, "Has it *done* anything?" Wesley may not have been so far wide of the mark when he raised the question with his preachers whether their preaching had converted anybody or angered anybody. At least he knew that preaching was intended to *do something!*

[8] Hjalmar Lindroth, *En Bok am Bibeln* (Lund: Gleerups Verlag, 1948), p. 191, in *Source Material Study*, No. 50G/112, World Council of Churches.

Sub-Christian Preaching

Now it is the nature of the Christian revelation as a historic Deed, and the fact that true preaching is actually a part of that Deed, which becomes the measuring rod by which all our preaching must be judged. Either we bear witness to the Deed, and by that witness the Deed is prolonged and made effective, or we do not preach. To comment on the times, no matter how incisively; to set forth a philosophy of life, no matter how effectively; to state, even, a theology, no matter how clearly; to moralize, no matter how winsomely—none of these is in essence Christian preaching. For these are not unique to Christianity. There are commentators, philosophers, theologians, moralizers, who bear no relation to the Christian faith at all. It is only as these are transformed in the broad context of reproducing the Deed of redemption that they can be Christianized.

This fact is strikingly put by H. H. Farmer, who reminds us that since Christianity is at heart an absolutely "unique, decisive, . . . final, completely adequate, wholly indispensable" Event, it could never have been discovered by human reflection, for reflection cannot produce an event. "An event can only establish itself—by happening! . . . And it can only become generally known by being borne witness to, by being proclaimed, by the story being told. The more unparalleled it is, the more, obviously, this is so." I quote at length Dr. Farmer's deductions from this fact with regard to preaching:

From the beginning, then, Christianity, being concerned with The Event which by definition has no parallel, God being agent in it as He is not in other happenings, was committed to preaching, to proclamation. Whoso said Christianity, said preaching. There was no choice between that and absolutely ceasing to be, with not the least chance of ever occurring again. It is theoretically conceivable that all the sacred books of Hinduism, and every Hindu, might be utterly destroyed, and yet substantially the same religion reappear. It is not very likely; but it is not a self-contradictory idea. Indeed it would fit harmoniously into the Hindu scheme of thought to suppose that if Hinduism vanished today it would reappear tomorrow, fifty years, a thousand years hence. But were all Christian records and all Christians extirpated, Christianity could not recur again. In its recurrence without a preacher, without a witness, it would flatly contradict all that it had always claimed to be. To put it paradoxically, in happening again it would show that it had never, according to its own definition of itself, happened at all.[9]

This means, therefore, that since the unique element in the Christian faith is the redemptive Deed, preaching is Christian only as it is oriented to that Deed and centered in it. And Christianity can be propagated only by *Christian* preaching.

The early church made much of this in their clear distinction between preaching, *kerygma,* and teaching, *didache.* C. H. Dodd says of this, "For the early Church to preach the Gospel was by no means the same thing as to deliver moral instruction or exhortation. While the Church was concerned to hand on the teaching of the Lord, it was not by this that it made converts. It was by *kerygma,* says Paul, not by *didache,* that it pleased God to save men." [10]

This distinction is a vital one, I believe, and one on which the true propagation of the Christian faith depends. For much that passes for the best preaching in our time could hardly be rated true preaching at all by this New Testament standard. An illustration may serve to sharpen the issue. A few years ago a preacher who was considered by many to be one of the great preachers of all time preached an Easter

[9] *The Servant of the Word.* Pp. 18-19. Used by permission of the publishers, Charles Scribner's Sons.
[10] *Op. cit.,* p. 8.

sermon on the passage in Psalm 138:8a (K.J.V.): "The Lord will perfect that which concerneth me." The stated theme of the sermon was that "God will not leave the universe at last filled with unfinished business. . . . God is not the God of unfinished business; the last word in this universe is not withheld completion. What God begins he carries through. In ourselves, in our friends, in this creative universe, in the supreme souls of the race and, above all, in Christ, he has started something. He does not light such candles merely to blow them out."

Now it is obvious to anyone who is even faintly familiar with the New Testament that such preaching as this has little, if anything, that is distinctively Christian about it. It is sheer philosophy that any theist could accept if he so desired, with no relation to the Christian faith whatsoever. Or even a nontheist, who felt that the universe is impersonally benevolent, might conceivably, by some sort of theory of the conservation of spiritual energy, accept the hope that all the values of human life will be conserved. In fact, the preacher himself seems to recognize this. He frankly says, "Indeed, leave God out for a moment and look at the universe itself. It is creative. A billion years ago, could one have seen the earth, who could have dreamed what would come of it? When life first appeared, who could have guessed to what heights it would rise in mind and character? Great things seem to be afoot in this creative cosmos." Then the preacher brings in the prophet H. G. Wells to prove it. "H. G. Wells is no sentimentalist," he cries, "but listen to him: 'All this world is heavy with the promise of greater things.'" Then another scientist is brought in to undergird the case, who says that there must be "something more than an endless procession of life out of and into the dark."

It is not caviling, but sober fact, to suggest that the early Christians would not have known they were in a Christian church if they had heard such preaching on Easter. The apostles had plenty of faith in God, but no deductions about the immortality of the soul based on that faith rekindled their blasted hopes following the Crucifixion. It was rather their personal encounter with the risen Lord which transformed their despair. This sermon rests the resurrection of Jesus—albeit only a spiritual resurrection—on the theory of the immortality of the soul. The early Christians moved in exactly the opposite direction. They rested the immortality of the Christian on the resurrection of Jesus. They did not believe that Jesus was alive because all good things are immortal. Rather, they believed that those who were "in Christ" were immortal because Jesus rose from the dead. "Because I live, you will live also" (John 14:19). It was "our Savior Christ Jesus, who abolished death and brought life and immortality to light through the gospel" (II Tim. 1:10). The idea of immortality for the Christian rested on the fact of the resurrection of Jesus Christ, not the reverse. Paul could not have written, "Since all good souls are immortal, we believe that Christ is alive." Rather, he wrote, "If Christ did not rise your faith is futile and your sins have never been forgiven. . . . But the glorious fact is that Christ *did* rise from the dead: He has become the very First to rise of all who sleep the sleep of death" (I Cor. 15:14, 20, Phillips). The ongoing life of Christ was not an idea based on the immortality of the soul, but was rather the result of an event which happened "on the third day" and was witnessed by many living believers. Assurance of the life eternal did not lie for the early Christians at the end of a syllogism, but in faith in the risen Jesus, who in his own resurrection had "abolished death."

28

Furthermore, faith which rests on conclusions to premises is subject to change without notice. Our ideas grow wobbly under the weight of events and cannot hold up the structure of our faith when life tumbles in with too great force. Christian assurance rests only on the unchanging Deed of redemption, which has already been achieved and cannot be undone, and will be consummated in God's own time. This is eloquently witnessed in the fact that when this sermon was preached fifteen years ago, H. G. Wells could be an apostle of such a faith. What was Wells's later view? The title of his last book, written not long before his death, is significant: *Mind at the End of Its Tether*.[11] What did he find when his short tether drew him up with a jar? Did he still believe that "all this world is heavy with the promise of greater things"? No, *homo sapiens* is "played out," and a "jaded world" is "devoid of recuperative power." There is "no pattern of things to come." The world "is like a convoy lost in darkness on an unknown rocky coast, with quarreling pirates in the chartroom and savages clambering up the sides of the ships to plunder and do evil as the whim may take them." [12]

This is not the place to quarrel with Wells's conclusions. It is the place, however, to indicate what disaster can overtake pious conclusions which rest on human hopes and reason, rather than on God's redemptive action in history. And it is the place to point out that a Christianity nurtured on preaching which is philosophy draped out in attractive religious garments will be brought up with a rough jerk at the end of its tether sooner than it expects, and could conceivably find its self-made God turning suddenly into the "harsh, implacable hostility" which Wells saw as the "Power" behind the cosmic process. Christian preachers are com-

[11] London: William Heinemann, Ltd., 1945.
[12] Cf. P. Carnegie Simpson, "The Last Words of H. G. Wells," *The British Weekly*, August 29, 1946, p. 294.

missioned for better things than brilliant surmises based on human hopes. They are to be heralds of the great redemptive Deed, already decisively accomplished in Jesus Christ and yet to be consummated when this age gives way to the age to come. But to herald this is to become a part of the Deed, to share, as Paul put it, in the "universal travail," the "painful tension" of hope through which "the whole of created life will be rescued from the tyranny of change and decay, and have its share in that magnificent liberty which can only belong to the children of God!" (Rom. 8:20-21, Phillips.) The preaching of the Cross, said Forsyth, is "part of the action of the Cross." The word of the Cross "is really the Cross's own energy, the Cross in action. . . . The real presence of Christ crucified is what makes preaching. It is what makes of a speech a sermon, and of a sermon Gospel." [13]

The New Testament Conception of Preaching

There is one more thing to say which undergirds this conception of preaching, and that is that such is the view of preaching set forth in the New Testament. Preaching, in the New Testament, is really God in action. In Peter's speech to Cornelius he speaks of *God* "preaching good news of peace by Jesus Christ" (Acts 10:36). He then mentions the life and mighty works of Jesus—his death, his resurrection, his exaltation to the position of Judge of the living and the dead, and his power to forgive sins. The total Christ-Deed was the preaching of God to men. God's preaching was to enact redemption.

If God's preaching was his redemptive action, then when men preached, they became the instruments whereby God continued to act redemptively. In Ephesians 2:17 the preaching of the apostles is described as the preaching of Christ.

[13] *Op. cit.*, p. 82.

In their preaching he was active, breaking down "the dividing wall of hostility" between Jew and Gentile, and reconciling "both to God in one body through the cross." Calvin remarks on this passage that the apostles preached "not only in his name, and by his command, but as it were *in his own person*," so that their preaching "is justly ascribed to none other than [Christ] himself."

Another passage which equates the preaching of the apostles with God's redemptive action is to be found in I Peter 1:23-25. There Peter speaks of the fact that his readers "have been born anew, not of perishable seed but of imperishable, through the living and abiding word of God." This word is the Logos, the Creator and Redeemer of the world. It is through him that they have been "born anew." But how was this new birth through the grace of the Redeemer effected? "The word referred to, as far as you are concerned," says Peter, "is the message of the gospel that was preached to you" (I Pet. 1:25, Phillips). Here the living Word which redeems is equated with the preached word which was the agent of its action. The preaching of the apostles was the Redeemer in action.

This same truth can be seen in I Thessalonians, where Paul describes the welcome the Thessalonians gave his preaching, and how they "turned to God from idols, to serve a living and true God, and to wait for his Son from heaven." This was accomplished, Paul says to them, because "when you received the word of God which you heard from us, you accepted it not as the word of men but as what it really is, the word of God, which is at work in you believers" (I Thess. 1:9, 10; 2:13).

But perhaps the most vivid statement of the conception of preaching as an actual participation in the Deed of redemption is to be seen in Paul's Letter to the Galatians. There he speaks of "placarding" Christ crucified before their eyes, or preaching Christ in such a way that the crucified one was as plainly set before their gaze as though they had stood before the cross itself. But the real meaning of Paul's ministry among the Galatians is to be seen in his word to them in 4:19, one of those undesigned, spontaneous statements which reveal things which no conscious effort could portray: "Oh my dear children, I feel the pangs of childbirth all over again till Christ be formed within you" (Phillips). What was his initial preaching among them? It was surely something more than a neat pattern of words. It was the pangs of childbirth through which Paul, participating in the agony of redemption, was striving to bring Christ to birth in the Galatians. And what could this have been but Christ himself, through Paul, bringing the power of his suffering love to bear upon their lives until they were born into the life of the kingdom of God?

The Supreme Importance of Preaching

If this is preaching, who can think of it lightly? If this is preaching, who can relegate it to an inferior position in the total range of his ministerial activity? If this is preaching, who can think of it as "a necessary evil"? There can be no activity in the world equal to it! To think that the redemptive Deed of God is to be brought to a focus in one's life as he stands before men in the act of preaching; that the yearning agony of the Redeemer is to leap into actuality on the plane of history once more; that the turning point of destiny for some soul, or some congregation, or even a significant turning point in history, for that matter, may be reached as one humbly but passionately proclaims the Word of God—this is an overwhelming realization which makes every other activity pale into insignificance.

32

Our day is waiting for a recovery of this New Testament understanding of the meaning and importance of preaching. Protestantism is not likely to rise much higher than the level of its pulpit. Romanism can survive without great preaching, but not Protestantism. And it is the failure of Protestants to understand the nature and function of preaching that makes them cast longing eyes toward Rome and indulge in the mimicry of altars, vestments, and pageantry which is invading Protestantism with alarming rapidity. The element of alarm lies not in any inherent wrong in these things but in the loss of the things which they replace. They are symptomatic of a hunger which they can meet only poorly. They are vain efforts to supply what must be met at a deeper level. We are not priests; we are prophets. We do not officiate at altars; we are living voices through whom Christ wants to speak. What the priest vainly *tries* to do in the Mass, our pulpits are given us to *do*.

Of this, Harris E. Kirk has written:

A point of consequence to observe is that, even in so potent a conception as the Roman mass, human nature is used as a means of communication of something divine. The consecrating words of the priest, according to that belief, convey to the material elements power to transform them into the body and blood of Christ. And upon this Deed of God is founded the experience of worship and communion.

But if such an experience is possible under these conditions, is it not more reasonable to believe that when a man is wholly given up to communicate the word of God, when he is engaged in preaching the gospel of salvation, he is actually participating in a sacramental act far more significant than that of the Roman mass? If by words man can ordain material symbols, how much more can this be accomplished by preaching the word of life? [14]

[14] *The Spirit of Protestantism* (New York and Nashville: Abingdon-Cokesbury Press, 1930), pp. 215-16. Used by permission.

The Romanist says, "When the priest pronounces the tremendous words of Consecration, he reaches up into the heavens, brings Christ down from his throne, and places him upon our altar to be offered up again as the victim for the sins of man." Protestantism, when it is true to its genius, does something better. When the Protestant preacher preaches—if he really preaches in the terms set forth here— the living Christ, who is always present in the fellowship of his people, both in heaven and on earth, expresses himself not in dumb symbol but in living reality, and offers once again to men the reconciliation with God once accomplished by his death and resurrection and now eternally available to all who will believe. Men do not see, through superstitious imagination, and as mute observers, a magical transformation of material symbols by the official intervention of a priest. They are confronted by the living Christ himself, who chooses to make his eternal redemptive Deed effectual by making the word of the preacher become His own word in the fellowship of the members of his body.

Dr. A. J. Gossip writes:

How often . . . we hear that stupid criticism of the Protestant form of worship, that it is too subjective, too man-centred; whereas, so we are assured, the glory of the Romanist type is that it is wisely God-centred and objective. All which is, surely, the exact opposite of the facts. In the Mass what is happening? Touched by the overflowing goodness and grace of God to him, man would like to be able to make some offering to the great and unwearied Giver, as a proof of his gratitude. But what can he present? All that he has is God's. And, not an item of it but has been soiled and rendered unworthy to be offered to the Holy One by the human sin that has polluted it. But there is Jesus Christ, in the splendour of His purity and perfection. And Him they seek to offer.

That is to say, that at the climax of their most holy hour, man is the central figure, as the officiating priest shows by the very way

34

he faces. He speaks as man's representative; he offers that tremendous offering in their name, on their behalf. The service is man-centred, in the sense that it is man who acts and gives. But at the climax of Protestant worship it is God who speaks and acts and gives, as the very way the minister is facing typifies. He is the representative, not merely of the people, but even more of God. . . . In the sermon it is God's word he brings. . . . As truly there as at the sacrament, it is Christ's hand offering hungry souls the bread of life. The service is God-centred. And Jesus Christ is in the midst.[15]

It is for this reason that Paul lists preaching the word of God as the supreme commission to the Church. When he lists, in I Corinthians 12, his various "manifestations of the Spirit for the common good," he places "the utterance of wisdom" and "the utterance of knowledge" prior to faith, gifts of healing, working of miracles, etc. And lest his order here should be considered casual, a few verses later he speaks of the different offices in the Corinthian church with explicit reference to his judgment of their importance. "God has appointed in the church first apostles, second prophets, third teachers, then workers in miracles, then healers, helpers, administrators, speakers in various kinds of tongues" (I Cor. 12:28). Here preaching, since both the apostles and the prophets were preachers, is set first in importance among all the functions of the minister. And Paul stresses this by adding, "But earnestly desire the higher gifts" (I Cor. 12:31).

This judgment of Paul's was merely a reflection of his own sense of mission. He had been commissioned to preach. "Woe to me if I do not preach the gospel!" (I Cor. 9:16.) God "who had set me apart before I was born, and had called me through his grace, was pleased to reveal his Son to me, in order that I might preach" (Gal. 1:15-16). "For Christ

[15] *In the Secret Place of the Most High* (New York: Charles Scribner's Sons, 1947), pp. 122-23. Used by permission of the publishers.

did not send me to baptize but to preach" (I Cor. 1:17.).

Carlyle once described teaching as "truth lighted at the flame of living truth." To pass out ideas is not to teach. The ideas must be incarnated in the life of the teacher, so that they leap like flame into the life of the student and incarnate themselves in him. We may paraphrase Carlyle by saying that preaching is "faith lighted at the flame of living faith." Truth must be incarnated in the life of the preacher, so that it leaps like flame into the life of the hearer, and reincarnates itself there. And since Christian truth is personal—"I am the truth"—incarnate truth in a Christian preacher is the incarnate Christ. To preach is not merely to *say* something, but to *do* something—it is to become the living arena in which Christ personally confronts men in judgment and redemption. Said Gregory Thaumaturgus of the preaching of Origen, "Like some spark it came dropping into my inmost soul. And there, being kindled and catching fire, was love: Love towards the Word Himself, most alluring to all by reason of beauty unspeakable, the holy, the most lovely." [16] Would you not rather preach like that than anything else in the world? Then Gregory commented, "The greatest gift this man has received from God, this portion wholly good is his from heaven, that he should be interpreter of the words of God to man, himself to explain the things of God as though it were God speaking." [17]

That is preaching. To speak *as though it were God speaking!* Not words, but a deed—the Deed of redemption! Therefore, preach! The world is waiting, and God is waiting, for men who are not content with mere sermons, but who know what it is to *preach*, and are willing, by God's grace, to strive to do it.

[16] Cf. John Foster, *After the Apostles* (London: SCM Press, 1951), p. 106. Used by permission of SCM Press and The Macmillan Co.

[17] *Ibid.*, p. 107. Used by permission.

CHAPTER II

The Role of the Bible in Preaching

IF what we have said thus far is true, that preaching is not the setting forth of religious ideas in acceptable form but the actualization of the historic Deed of redemption in the present moment, then the conviction of this chapter inevitably arises: namely, the place to go for one's sermons is to the record of that redemptive Deed—the Bible. The abiding record of that unique Event forms the starting point for every effort at reproducing it in human experience.

Contemporary Neglect of the Bible in Preaching

This sounds almost like a truism, but it is not so accepted if the practice of most modern preachers one hears is any criterion. The custom seems to be to get sermons out of the general treasure of one's own ideas or the best current thought on religious questions, and then, after the sermon is prepared, to search for an appropriate text to attach to it. Or, if the process begins with the text, there is little or no effort to find out what the text means in the light of the passage of which it is a part and in relation to the broad sweep of the history of redemption set forth in the Bible. The text is more often used as a self-starter for the preacher's own thoughts, which, like the starter on a car, immediately drops out of the picture the moment the motor begins to run. Someone has said that if texts were smallpox, most modern preachers would never contract the disease!

A student inadvertently furnished a good illustration of this several years ago. He called me on the telephone on Saturday evening to say that he had just finished a sermon for the next day but had not been able to find an appropriate text for it, and he wondered whether I would be kind enough to help him find a text. He then proceeded to rehearse the sermon so that I would have an adequate basis on which to make a selection. My initial reaction—which Christian restraint forbade me from voicing—was to say, "Use almost any text. If your sermon is already prepared without making any study of a scripture passage, it makes little difference what text you use." My second reaction—likewise unvoiced —was, "Why use a text at all? If you are preaching your own thoughts, why not just set them forth as such and not blame them on the Bible by appending a text to your remarks?" If this were an isolated instance, it would be amusing. The seriousness of it, however, lies in the fact that one could multiply instance after instance of the very same thing in the preaching of mature, highly reputable ministers whose sermons betray a lack of any vital connection whatsoever with the texts on which they are allegedly based.

An example of this was given by R. W. Dale when he told of a very eminent minister in England preparing a very fine sermon on some words which he imagined were in the book of Proverbs. Before leaving for church on Sunday morning, the minister decided that it would be well to look up the exact reference of his text. Upon leafing through Proverbs he could not find it. In desperation, he turned to Cruden's *Concordance,* but could not find it listed there. So when the moment came for beginning to preach, he said something to this effect: "You will remember, my friends, the words of the wisest of kings"—and then took off on the sermon he had prepared as though nothing unusual had occurred. Dr. Dale commented: "I think that my friend would have done better if he had warned the people that though he thought the words were Solomon's, he had not been able to find them, even with the help of a concordance. He discovered afterwards, I think, that the words were in one of the collects or prayers of the Anglican Prayerbook." [1] On the basis of this incident, Dale felt it necessary to counsel young preachers what normally would seem to be a ridiculous thing: "When you take a text be sure that it is in the Bible!" [2] The fact that such counsel as this ever needs to be given is more than amusing—it is tragic!

The Uniqueness of the Bible

The root of the difficulty here is the same as that which makes ministers take a low view of their preaching: namely, a failure to understand what preaching is as it was described in the first chapter. If preaching is the setting forth of religious ideas through the arts of effective speech, then of course one may preach a "good" sermon with no serious wrestling with the Bible. If, on the other hand, true preaching is a function of God whereby the agony of the divine redemption is brought to a focus through a man in the act of preaching, it seems reasonable that the fountain source of this will be the record of the divine action in history by which God achieved our redemption.

The uniqueness of the redemptive Deed is what gives to the Bible its uniqueness. If the Bible were merely, as many think, the record of man's growing religious consciousness,

[1] *Nine Lectures on Preaching* (New York: George H. Doran Co., 1878), p. 125.
[2] *Ibid.*

then it is not unique, even though we may regard it as on a higher level than other similar records. Furthermore, if the revelation in the Bible were primarily ideas rather than action, religious truths rather than the redemptive Deed of God, then it is possible to supersede it and rightly to find the source of our preaching elsewhere. To this C. W. Dugmore calls attention when, in criticizing the position taken by William Sanday a couple of generations ago in his Bampton Lectures on "Inspiration," he writes: "If all that 'has come down to us is Revelation, *i.e.* a number of concrete truths contained in written books on the subject of God and religion' . . . , it is hard to see why the particular anthology of 'concrete truths about God and religion,' which we call the Bible, should not now be revised and considerably enlarged from the writings of men in subsequent ages." [3] A. G. Hebert, in further drawing out the implications of this, adds that on this view "it may even seem to be a matter for regret" that "many parts of the Bible" are "in the Bible at all, and the Bible would be better without them. Nor can it be denied that some books which are in the Bible compare not too favourably with books which are outside it; thus on the whole Esther is less edifying than Ecclesiasticus, and Jude than I Clement—not to speak of St. Augustine's Confessions." [4]

Why not preach from Augustine, or Aquinas, or Calvin, or Rufus Jones, or Frank Laubach, as well as the Bible? If the heart of the Bible lies in its religious truths, there would seem to be nothing incongruous in this. The over-enthusiastic Methodist minister would then have been correct in declaring to a gathering of ministers that Bishop Mc-

[3] *The Interpretation of the Bible* (London: Society for Promoting Christian Knowledge, 1946), p. *viii*.
[4] *The Authority of the Old Testament* (London: Faber and Faber, Ltd., 1947), p. 36. Used by permission.

Connell knew more about God than did Isaiah! (I am sure that the bishop would have been the first one to eliminate himself from the competition!) If the prophecy of Isaiah exists now merely to give us ideas about God, then it would indeed be surprising if men, after witnessing the incarnation of Jesus Christ, did not have some ideas superior to those of a prophet of the eighth century B.C. But if the prophecy of Isaiah is a part of an unfolding divine drama in which God himself was the chief actor on the stage of history, then it abides today, and shall always abide, as a witness to the particular scene in this unique drama which unfolded in Isaiah's particular period of history. And its abiding value lies not merely in the number or richness of its ideas, but in the indispensable part it plays in making intelligible the final outcome of the drama in the coming of Jesus Christ. It is because of the truth expressed by Suzanne de Dietrich when she says that "one can say without any difference that the Bible is the Word of God or that it is the *Book of the Acts of God*," [5] that we claim uniqueness for the Bible and plead that true preaching can have no other source than the witness which the Bible bears to the divine redemptive action. The Bible is "the fountain of its faith," and the church cannot expect rivers of living water to flow from its pulpits unless these draw primarily and continually on the fountain.

The Bible as the Preacher's Charter

It is my own high conviction that the only right a man has to stand in a pulpit before a gathered congregation of men and presume to declare the living word of the living God by which he creates eternal life in the souls of men and makes them members of the new Israel, is that he is

[5] *Le Dessein de Dieu* (Neuchatel: Delachaux et Niestlé, 1948), p. 8.

making an honest effort to bear witness to what he has found in the Bible. For this the Protestant pulpit exists. The very symbolism of the open Bible on the pulpit before the minister is an abiding reminder of the fact that the preacher stands before men as an interpreter of holy scripture, as a catalytic agent by which the redemption recorded in the Bible and the need for redemption in the human heart shall be brought together in a mighty fusion.

The symbolism of certain Reformed churches in Europe is even more striking. There the Bible, instead of lying open on the pulpit before the preacher, lies open before the congregation in front of the pulpit, as though the business of the preacher is to aid the worshipers rightly to read the Word of God for themselves, so that the Deed there recorded shall leap into life for them. The preacher is an interpreter standing behind the Bible, leading the people into a living encounter with the redemptive God whose action in history is there set forth, action which he wants to reproduce in the lives of men now. "The Bible," to quote Suzanne de Dietrich again, "does not speak to us *about God,* but *in the name of God.*" [6] If we, therefore, would speak to men *in the name of God,* which alone is true preaching, we must speak out of the Bible.

Jesus' Use of the Old Testament

Striking evidence to undergird this view is to be seen in Jesus' use of the Old Testament. If anyone ever had the right to cut himself loose from the Bible and launch out on his own, it was Jesus. And yet Jesus never once dreamed of doing anything but interpreting the Old Testament, both in his teaching and, supremely, in his life. I recall reading somewhere the judgment that Jesus was not an expository preacher. The writer took this position in trying to defend the deity of Jesus, suggesting that since he was divine, he did not need to draw his truth from the Bible, but declared the mind of God directly perceived by him. Such a view runs entirely counter to the evidence of the New Testament. An examination of the Gospels indicates that Jesus not only used the Old Testament as a source for his preaching, but that it became the touchstone of his whole life.

Jesus' use of the Old Testament did not lie in choosing from it a few texts of rare beauty as a basis for his ethical teaching, nor even in finding a few predictions to be fulfilled with more or less mechanical faithfulness. Rather, he felt that all that God had been doing in history from the beginning was now being consummated in him. The divine purpose of salvation which had been carried forward in all God's acts with his people was now in him to be achieved. The old exodus by which the old Israel had been constituted a people was in him to be fulfilled in a new and greater exodus by which Israel would be reconstituted into a New Israel in which all nations were to be included; the old covenant was to find its true meaning in the New Covenant to which Jeremiah had looked forward, written on the tables of men's hearts; the old sacrifices were to be gathered up in the one supreme Sacrifice toward which they had been pointing, the sacrifice of himself on the cross. *Jesus' whole life became one grand exposition of the entire Old Testament,* by a series of profound correspondences. All the acts of God in the whole of history were to be gathered up in the one great Act. He was bringing to a climax the drama of redemption. Through him the plot would be resolved, the earlier scenes would find their meaning, and God, the Actor, would complete his role in history by the climactic enactment of a Tragedy great enough to match the tragedy of the human scene. The one thread which binds all the thought and behavior of Jesus together is his supreme awareness that the divine action in the Old Testament was coming to its completion in him. This is such a marked feature of Jesus' thought that a reputable Swedish scholar has recently made the statement that "the Old Testament is, properly speaking, *the* Bible, even for the Christian Church, and that the New Testament is, if one may say so, nothing but a little appendix containing a list of strange words (in the Old Testament) which need explanation." [7] After this view was challenged, he replied: "Now I admit that the formulation of my thesis was somewhat provocative. But the more I read and thought about it, the more I became convinced of its striking truth." [8] Even if this should be an overstatement, it at least indicates that the Old Testament was *the* Bible to Jesus, and that since he found the meaning and pattern of his own life there, we must go there to understand him ourselves.

An examination of some relevant passages will serve to make clear how inextricably rooted Jesus was in the Old Testament. In the struggle to determine the main features of his mission as he launched his public career, the issue was finally settled for Jesus by the voice at the Baptism, a voice which did nothing other than bring together two strands of messianic prophecy from the Old Testament. In the temptation experience which followed, Jesus' problem was to relate the mission of Suffering Servant which he had accepted to other strands of Old Testament teaching which on the surface seemed to run counter to it. The whole scene, which obviously had to come from Jesus himself, was a mighty conflict in the soul of Jesus to understand the role

[7] A. A. van Ruler, *Religie en Politiek*, quoted in Study 51E/125, May, 1951 (Geneva: Study Department, World Council of Churches), p. 7.
[8] *Ibid.*

he was to play in climaxing the divine drama of redemption set forth in the Old Testament. The public declaration of his mission at his home-town synagogue very early in his career is given in this form:

And he stood up to read; and there was given to him the book of the prophet Isaiah. He opened the book and found the place where it was written,

"The Spirit of the Lord is upon me,
because he has anointed me to preach good news to the poor."
. . . .

And he closed the book, and gave it back to the attendant, and sat down. . . . And he began to say to them, "Today this scripture has been fulfilled in your hearing" (Luke 4:16-18, 20-21).

He then proceeded to enforce his thought by dwelling on Old Testament incidents gathering around Elijah and Elisha. When he was requested by the people at Capernaum to stay with them, he replied, "I must preach the good news of the kingdom of God to the other cities also; for I was sent for this purpose" (Luke 4:43). The "kingdom of God" could be no other than the kingdom promised in the Old Testament, and Jesus conceived his mission to be the realization of that promise.

In the Sermon on the Mount, Jesus said: "Think not that I have come to abolish the law and the prophets; I have come not to abolish them but to fulfil them" (Matt. 5:17). And when he added several times, "You have heard that it was said. . . . But I say to you," he was not doing away with the Law nor making himself independent of it, but was merely laying down the high demand for righteousness inherent in the Law rightly understood. As Hoskyns and Davey put it, "The Righteousness which Jesus demanded

45

. . . was the demand of God revealed to the Hebrew people." [9] And wherever the Old Testament is declared superseded, an appeal is always made to the Old Testament itself to validate the declaration. When Jesus, therefore, set aside certain aspects of the Old Testament he found his authority to do so because the Old Testament itself summed up the Law in its two precepts, one in Deuteronomy and the other in Leviticus—"You shall love the Lord your God with all your heart, and with all your soul, and with all your mind. This is the great and first commandment. And a second is like it, You shall love your neighbor as yourself. On these two commandments depend all the law and the prophets" (Matt. 22:37-40).

When John sent from prison asking, "Are you he who is to come, or shall we look for another?" (Luke 7:19), Jesus replied by setting his work in the framework of the Old Testament, referring John to two passages in the prophecy of Isaiah. He then proceeded to interpret John's mission to the multitudes in terms of Malachi's promise of Elijah's coming. When Jesus claimed lordship over the Sabbath, he referred to David and to the behavior of the Old Testament priests on the Sabbath as the basis of his own actions (Luke 6:3 ff.). His introduction of the use of parables is justified by a lengthy quotation from Isaiah indicating that God's problem of dealing with an unresponsive people in the days of Isaiah was being faced once more and supremely in Jesus (Matt. 13:14 ff.). At the Great Confession, Jesus accepted Peter's affirmation that he was the Jewish Messiah (Matt. 16:16). In the announcement to the disciples of his suffering, he was inaugurating them into a conception of his mission as that of the Suffering Servant of the Old Testament (Matt. 16:21).

[9] *The Riddle of the New Testament* (New York: Harcourt, Brace & Co., 1931), p. 195. Used by permission.

At the Transfiguration a week later, there appeared unto him Moses and Elijah, representing the Law and the Prophets, who spoke with him concerning his "exodus" which he was to accomplish at Jerusalem (Luke 9:31). In his triumphal entry into Jerusalem, Jesus deliberately dramatized an Old Testament passage in Zechariah (Matt. 21:4 ff.). In cleansing the Temple, he was asserting his authority as Jewish Messiah in the Temple.[10] At his Last Supper with his disciples, as he took the cup and passed it to them, he said, "This is my blood of the covenant," thus setting his death in focal relation to the New Covenant which he was enacting as the climax of the old covenant (Matt. 26:28). In the supreme moment of his agony on the cross, Jesus' consciousness found expression in the twenty-second psalm (Matt. 27:46). Then after the Resurrection, when he met the disciples on the road to Emmaus, he upbraided them, " 'O foolish men, and slow of heart to believe all that the prophets have spoken!' . . . And beginning with Moses and all the prophets, he interpreted to them in all the scriptures the things concerning himself" (Luke 24:25, 27). When the disciples told of it later, they said, "Did not our hearts burn within us while he talked to us on the road, *while he opened to us the scriptures?*" (Luke 24:32, italics mine.)

This survey of passages is very partial, and it could be extended at length to indicate that at every turn of Jesus' life he felt that he was under the control of an eternal purpose which had been working itself out on the stage of history, and which was to reach its climax in him. "The uniqueness of the obedience of Jesus," wrote Hoskyns and Davey, was "dictated by a creative and penetrating insight into the meaning of the Old Testament Scriptures. . . . This

---

[10] Cf. E. F. Scott, *The Crisis in the Life of Jesus* (New York: Charles Scribner's Sons, 1952), for a recent and most helpful study of this crucial incident in Jesus' career.

was the conscious purpose which lay behind and conditioned His words and actions." [11] "Jesus acted as He did act and said what He did say because He was consciously fulfilling a necessity imposed upon Him by God through the demands of the Old Testament." [12]

If this be true, how then can we expect to interpret the meaning of Jesus or be the agents of bringing his redemptive Deed to bear upon the lives of men unless we begin where he began—with the Bible? If Jesus was conscious in every act that he was fulfilling a destiny set down for him in the history of Israel, how can that destiny be understood save through our setting his life and death and resurrection in the framework of that same history? It is our failure to do this which moves our preaching so often out of the tremendous throb of vital accomplishment in the historic Deed of redemption and allows it to trail off into vapid moralism and religious ethical culture. The conclusion here seems inescapable, that if Jesus' whole life was one long exposition of holy scripture, then our preaching of him must likewise be an exposition of scripture.

The Old Testament in the New Testament

In pressing such a judgment as this, it is heartening to find it undergirded by the writers of the New Testament themselves. A thorough look at the New Testament indicates that they shared the view of Jesus that the meaning of what he had done for them was to be understood in the light of God's action recorded in the Old Testament. They were members of the fellowship which had been created by the mighty Act of Jesus. They felt surging through their corporate life a tremendous dynamic which drove them out to capture every frontier of life for Jesus, their Lord. But how

[11] *Op. cit.*, pp. 252-53. Used by permission.
[12] *Ibid.*, p. 160.

did they do it? By merely preaching Jesus? No, *they preached Jesus as the fulfillment of the Old Testament Scriptures.*

It is impossible to touch the New Testament at any significant spot without at the same time touching a vital nerve of the Old Testament. The very first words that are recorded on Christian lips after the ascension of Jesus are Peter's words to the gathered one hundred and twenty in the upper room: "Brethren, the scripture had to be fulfilled" (Acts 1:16). Then in his first sermon on the Day of Pentecost, after a sentence to gain the attention of the crowd, Peter said, "This is what was spoken by the prophet Joel," and then proceeded to quote at length from this prophecy (Acts 2:16 ff.). Then he added that the crucifixion of Jesus was "according to the definite plan and foreknowledge of God," and ended by setting the Resurrection in relation to certain Old Testament psalms. Peter's second recorded sermon at the Beautiful Gate follows a similar pattern. "The God of Abraham and of Isaac and of Jacob, the God of our fathers, glorified his servant Jesus," he affirmed (Acts 3:13). Then later he added, "But what God foretold by the mouth of all the prophets, that his Christ should suffer, he thus fulfilled" (Acts 3:18). Following that, the rest of the sermon is one clear setting forth of the fact that what had happened in Jesus was the establishment of "all that God spoke by the mouth of his holy prophets from of old" (Acts 3:21). When Peter addressed the Sanhedrin after his first arrest, he quoted Psalm 118, "This is the stone which was rejected by you builders, but which has become the head of the corner" (Acts 4:11). When, after his release, he joined the others, they prayed together, finding words to express their sense of the meaning of that moment in the second psalm (Acts 4:25 ff.). Follow on through the book of Acts—Stephen's address, Peter's rebuke of Simon Magus, Philip's experience with the Ethiopian eunuch, Paul's early preaching in Damascus, Peter's sermon in the home of Cornelius, Paul's sermon at Antioch of Pisidia, the Council of Jerusalem, Paul's preaching at Corinth, the preaching of Apollos at Corinth—time would fail us to mention more. Nor does the point need further elaboration, that the preaching of Jesus by the early church, as it is recorded in the book of Acts, is shot through and through with the Old Testament. Jesus was to them not the founder of a new religion but the consummation of God's historic dealings with Israel.

This same phenomenon is to be seen in the Gospels and the Epistles, both openly and subtly. Mark, the earliest of the Gospels, begins: "The beginning of the gospel of Jesus Christ, the Son of God. As it is written in Isaiah the prophet" (Mark 1:1-2). The first words ascribed in Mark to Jesus are: "The time is fulfilled, and the kingdom of God is at hand" (1:15). What time? Obviously, the time toward which the divine dealings in the Old Testament had been pointing. What is the kingdom of God? Obviously, it is the kingdom foreshadowed and promised in the Old Testament. What is the meaning of Jesus Christ? The name has no meaning whatsoever apart from the Old Testament. The simplest beginnings of an understanding of Jesus, therefore, rest squarely on his relation to the Old Testament. To follow all three of the Synoptic Gospels through in detail is impossible here, not to mention the Johannine writings or the letters of Paul or Hebrews or the Petrine epistles. But works such as Hoskyns and Davey, *The Riddle of the New Testament,* or A. G. Hebert, *The Authority of the Old Testament,* or R. V. G. Tasker's *The Old Testament in the New Testament,*[13] furnish striking evidence that the New Testament writers, without exception, were "concerned to show that

[13] Philadelphia: The Westminster Press, 1947.

50

the Life and Death of Jesus are intelligible only in the context of the Old Testament Scriptures." [14] Hebert sums it up:

> Indeed, there was no possibility of explaining who Jesus was, and what was the significance of His preaching and above all of His death and resurrection, and what was the true status of the Christian community, apart from the Old Testament Scriptures. It is scarcely an exaggeration to say that whenever a New Testament writer quotes or alludes to the Old Testament, it is in order to exhibit some aspect or other of the Divine Purpose that had been fulfilled in Jesus. . . . [The Old Testament] is God's Book, the record of His ordering of history in preparation for His own coming to accomplish His purpose of salvation; therefore it gives the indispensable key to the understanding of the Divine Advent which has now taken place.[15]

It is significant, too, that this incessant use of the Old Testament was not confined to the church's approach to the Jews alone, but the church's preaching to the Gentiles reflects the same effort to set Jesus in the framework of the Old Testament. Paul stated this clearly in the closing paragraph of the Epistle to the Romans, when he spoke of "the preaching of Jesus Christ, according to the revelation of the mystery which was kept secret for long ages but is now disclosed and *through the prophetic writings* is made known to *all nations*" (16:25-26, italics mine). Neither Jew nor Gentile could understand Jesus in any other way than "through the prophetic writings." Nor can it be said that this view of Jesus as the fulfillment of the redemptive purpose of God set forth in the Old Testament was imposed on the records by the early church. The late Théo Preiss, of Montpellier, France, remarked how strange it is that scholars should think of Peter, John, Paul, James, and all the rest as theologians who read their theology into the life of Jesus, without

---

[14] Hoskyns and Davey, *op. cit.*, p. 88. Used by permission.
[15] *Op. cit.*, pp. 200, 202. Used by permission.

seeing that Jesus himself may have been the supreme theologian who was the creative mind behind all New Testament thought. The best critical study has made it increasingly clear that the clue to the meaning of Jesus' life the church got from Jesus himself.[16]

The Bible and the Early Church

The New Testament writers' use of the Old Testament was the pattern which the early church fathers followed. In preaching to pagan people, their chief concern was to show that Jesus was God's crowning work in a long process of historical action which preceded him. When one remembers how scarce books were in the first three centuries, and how few must have been the available copies either of the Hebrew or Greek Old Testament, "it may well seem amazing," says John Foster, "that there is no single Apology we know, which does not refer to the scriptures, and either call men to search the scriptures for themselves, or preach Christianity to men from scriptural texts." [17] The early apologists sometimes made what we could call fanciful use of the Scriptures, often proof-texting from passages which the heathen little knew and in a way which to those who knew them could at times hardly have been convincing. But, as Foster continues, "With Justin, and preachers as early as he, there is this much to be said: They seek a scriptural basis for what they are saying, especially for what they are saying about Jesus Christ." [18] The extent of the range of their use of the Scriptures as background for their presentation of Jesus may be seen in the following passage from Justin Martyr:

[16] See, for example, William Manson, *Jesus the Messiah* (Philadelphia: The Westminster Press, 1946).

[17] *After the Apostles* (London: SCM Press, Ltd., 1951), pp. 73-74. Used by permission of SCM Press and The Macmillan Co.

[18] *Ibid., p.* 77. Used by permission.

We will now produce the proof, not taking it on trust from those who say so, but being inevitably persuaded by those who prophesied before it came to pass, since we see with our eyes things happened, and happening, just as they were foretold. This, we think, will seem to you also the best and truest evidence. . . . In these Books of the Prophets we find announced as coming, one born of a Virgin; and growing to manhood; and healing every disease and sickness and raising the dead; and being hated, disowned, and crucified—Jesus our Christ; and dying and rising again, and ascending into heaven, both being, and being called, Son of God; and certain sent by Him to every race of men to preach these things, and its being the men from the Gentiles rather, who believe in Him.[19]

The point here is not whether Justin and the others made proper use of the Old Testament in each instance. Their witness cannot be set aside with a smile at their fanciful interpretations. The point is that they, following exactly in the footsteps of the apostolic writers, had a profound awareness that Jesus was not a mere Teacher of religious ideas whose thought they were determined to perpetuate. He was, rather, the supreme Event in the unfolding of God's redemptive purpose through the ages, and as such he drew all the threads of the Old Testament together into a pattern of meaning which completed it, while it in turn explained him. It was folly to them, then, to try to understand Jesus save through the Old Testament.

The Bible Normative for all Preaching

Now all this that we have been dealing with took place before the formation of the New Testament canon. But the New Testament is simply the written record of what the early church believed and preached about Jesus. Hence, if in their preaching about him they made such large use of the

---

[19] Quoted by Foster, *op. cit.*, p. 77. Used by permission.

Old Testament, so now in proclaiming the truth which is recorded in the New Testament, we too must relate it to the Old Testament. The Old Testament and the New Testament together, therefore, become the only adequate source of our preaching, if Jesus, the apostles, the writers of the New Testament, and the early church fathers have any authentic guidance to offer us. And this is supremely so because of that on which we have been insisting, that the gospel of Jesus Christ is primarily a Deed, and every religious idea we hold about Jesus must be related to that Deed to have any truly Christian meaning. If any other method is adopted, said Hoskyns and Davey,

We might picture a religious personality who taught the "Brotherhood of Men" and the "Fatherhood of God"; or we might roughly sketch an ethical system on the basis of a few aphorisms, and suppose that Jesus was a teacher of Ethical Principles; or we might sketch the career of a reformer of Jewish piety; or we might discover a religious mystic, or disclose a man possessed of intense spiritual insight depending upon a peculiar religious experience; or indeed, by piecing together a different selection of fragments; we might equally well describe the Epiphany of a Divine Person who at no point touched human life as we know it. But these would be, not historical reconstructions, but simply selections of what seems to us convenient, or edifying, or useful, or monstrous.

An historical reconstruction is possible only when the uniform nature of the whole material at our disposal is perceived, so that each fragment is seen not only to be a part of the whole, but to contain the whole.[20]

And this means the whole redemptive Deed set forth in the Bible. A whole Christ can be had only out of a whole Bible. A whole gospel can be preached only out of a whole Bible.

[20] *Op. cit.*, pp. 248-49. Used by permission.

The Bible as Redemptive Deed

Two questions must yet be faced, the first of which has been touched upon briefly above. Why, in the light of the developing Christian church, does the Bible remain unique and authoritative for preaching? Why is the canon closed and a clear line of demarcation drawn between the history of redemption in the Bible and church history? The answer to this is to be seen in the light of the fact that revelation lies primarily in the unfolding drama of redemptive history, rather than in a set of religious ideas. Since the Bible is the record of the redemptive history, it remains permanently normative, even though under the guidance of the Holy Spirit the church should in subsequent times gain clearer insight into the full implications of that redemptive history. There is a profound sense in which the Scriptures are actually a part of the redemptive Deed of Christ. His Deed was to effect a new Exodus and to call a new Israel into being, an Israel which would transcend the narrow limits of the old Israel and include all nations. The creation of this new Israel, the church, therefore, was itself a part of the redemptive Deed once for all done by Christ. And even the gathering of the Gentiles into that church under the ministry of Paul was the completion of the Deed, and thus a part of it. Since the New Testament is the record of the creation of the church and the inclusion of the Gentiles, that record may be considered as a part of the unrepeatable Deed, and therefore unique.

The ongoing church, said Paul, is "built upon the foundation of the apostles and prophets" (Eph. 2:20). The building may grow and even be modified indefinitely, but the foundation cannot change. The original witnesses to the Resurrection and to the creation of the church are forever set apart as unique from all subsequent generations of Christians.

Jesus' word to Thomas in John 20, "Blessed are those who have not seen and yet believe," indicates that all who come after those who had "seen" stand in a different category, believing on the basis of the witness of the original group. The New Testament, then, as the record of their unique witness to Jesus as the climax of the Deed of redemption enacted throughout the Old Testament history, belongs to the Deed and shares in its uniqueness. Old and New Testaments belong together as the unified record of God's unique action. The record of the life, death, and resurrection of Jesus is meaningless without the witness of the Old Testament; likewise, the Old Testament remains an enigma without the witness of the New.

Hanson and Harvey suggest this in a striking illustration:

In some of the greatest musical compositions, of which the Overture to Wagner's opera, "The Mastersingers," is a very good example, many more themes than one are used by the composer. At first each theme is expressed and developed to some extent separately. Later, perhaps, two of the themes are combined in harmony, or alternate with each other. Finally, the climax is so arranged that all the themes, which were expressed before, are united and played simultaneously, strings, brass, woodwind and so on, each playing a theme, but the whole fitted together and the themes rearranged so as to harmonize in the final movement. To hear the end, the climax, by itself may be beneficial, but it is only when each theme has been perceived and understood while it was being first played that the fulfilment of all the themes together is seen in its true light and the wonder of it fully appreciated.
. . . The Old Testament is the development of separate themes. Christ is the climax and conclusion. The climax cannot really be understood apart from the previous part, the beginning, . . . and the themes cannot be fully understood until they are seen as . . . written beforehand so as to fit into the harmony of the climax to the whole work. For Christians the climax is the

achievement of the Incarnate Redeemer, Jesus Christ the son of God.[21]

The whole Bible, therefore, stands as the unique record of the unique history of redemption on which the subsequent life of the church is built. It remains forever, therefore, the unchanging and unchangeable source and norm of the continuing development of the church throughout all generations. As such it, and it alone, can rightly form the basis of all Christian preaching.

The Bible and Tradition

The second question is merely another phase of the first one: what is the relation of the Bible to tradition? Which is authoritative in interpreting the Christian faith, the Bible or the church? The traditional Protestant view, of course, has been that the Bible is superior to the tradition of the church and in all matters is the supreme and final court of appeal. The Roman Church has consistently challenged this, which is quite understandable, but in recent days there have been many Protestants going over to the Roman position. The great French liberal Protestant, Maurice Goguel, for example, says that it is impossible for us to set the Bible and tradition over against each other as the Reformers did, because we now know that the Bible was formulated by the early tradition of the church, and itself is a part of that tradition. If this be true, then there is no finality about the Bible, and there would seem to be little reason why the continuing development of the church should not enlarge or improve or replace the Bible.

The theological answer to this has already been made. However much the New Testament reflects the growth of a

[21] *The Loom of God* (Dublin and Belfast: Association for Promoting Christian Knowledge, 1945), pp. 79-80. Used by permission.

tradition, that growth itself is controlled by a common conviction about what has happened in Jesus Christ. "The delicate threads which hold together the New Testament," wrote Hoskyns and Davey,

have been shown to be converging upon one single point. Evangelists, Editors, Theologians; narratives of miracles, records of parables, collections of sayings; argumentation, discourses, controversies; difficult problems in textual criticism, subtle changes in the meanings of words; all this varied material concentrates upon and has its origin in one single, isolated, historical Event.[22]

This indicates that the revelation of God in the historic Event of Jesus controlled the development of the tradition within the New Testament at every point. Hence, even if the New Testament is a part of the tradition, the central core which controls its development is unique, and since the New Testament is the only place where that central core is set forth, that would make this unifying element in the New Testament the final, authoritative norm of Christian faith. Granted, therefore, that the church developed the canon, it did not thereby take precedence over it. It merely manifested its acceptance of the central core of reality in the Bible under the authority of which it lived its life.

Besides the theological answer, there is a historical answer to this question. If tradition is authoritative, why was a canon of holy scripture ever formed? It is historically plain that the early church, in developing a canon of scripture at all, was fully aware that she herself was not the infallible organ of the Holy Spirit. Had that been the case, she would have left the canon open, so that other works could periodically have been added. But in making a closed canon, as the late Théo Preiss wrote, the church

[22] *The Riddle of the New Testament* (New York: Harcourt, Brace & Co., 1931), pp. 248-49. Used by permission.

recognized once for all as being above itself certain writings of the apostolic epoch. She recognized then in the apostolic epoch an authority superior to her own. . . . It is evident that the church, in a chronological order, preceded the canon. But the temporal order is one thing, the real order is another. It is one thing to give, to confer an authority, it is another thing to recognize it.[23]

Historically, it was neither the Bible which produced the church nor the church which produced the Bible. They were both the products of the gospel, the one good message of redemption. But as the church got farther and farther away from the historic events which formed the heart of the gospel, she recognized in the scriptures which were canonized the authentic witness to those events out of which she was born and by which her life had to be nurtured. So, as Cullmann has concluded, in forming a closed canon the church "made the decisive distinction between the ancient tradition, which was now codified as Scripture, and the now beginning *further* tradition, which was to be controlled and judged on the basis of that earlier one. . . . This step could have no other meaning than that the Church thereby placed the Scripture over all tradition that might develop after that time." [24]

This control of the tradition by the Scriptures is foreshadowed in the Scriptures themselves. In the upper-room discourse in the Fourth Gospel, Jesus says that "the Holy Spirit, whom the Father will send in my name, he will teach you all things, and bring to your remembrance all that I have said to you. . . . He will not speak on his own authority, . . . for he will take what is mine and declare it to you" (John

[23] *Le Témoignage Intérieur du Saint-Esprit* (Neuchatel: Delachaux et Niestlé, 1946), p. 11.

[24] *Christ and Time*, tr. Floyd V. Filson (Philadelphia: The Westminster Press, 1950), pp. 170-71. See also Cullmann's article "Scripture and Tradition," *Scottish Journal of Theology*, June, 1953, pp. 113 ff.

14:26; 16:13, 14). Here the work of the Holy Spirit in guiding the church "into all the truth" is nothing other than a deepening of the church's apprehension and a broadening of its application of the things the historic Jesus said and did. To refer once more to a word of Théo Preiss:

The inner testimony of the Holy Spirit does not raise us proudly above the letter of the Word, but, on the contrary, having made us understand it a little, it stimulates us to submit ourselves to it all the more to know it better. The interior testimony, then, sends the believer back to the exterior testimony, which alone is normative. It adds nothing to the written revelation.[25]

The historic Event is normative for whatever advances the church is to make under the leadership even of the Holy Spirit.

Add to this the care with which the canon was formed, and the church's insistence that it represent the apostolic testimony; the insistence of the church that the one chosen to replace Judas should be one who has "accompanied us during all the time that the Lord Jesus went in and out among us, beginning from the baptism of John until the day when he was taken up from us" (Acts 1:21-22); the evidence that Paul, although he insisted that he did not receive his gospel from men, yet rooted his own preaching in the historic facts of Jesus' life; the concern that Paul had to verify the fact that he was actually a witness to the resurrection of Jesus, as were the other apostles. Then, by contrast, note how soon the developing tradition which was not controlled by the scriptures began to depart from the heart of the Christian faith, such as in the apocryphal New Testament writings. The conclusion becomes almost over-

[25] *Op. cit.*, p. 12.

whelming that the conviction of the Reformers that the Bible was the supreme authority for the church was indisputably right, as a return to the view held by the early church.

The Bible and Preaching

Every avenue of approach to the problem we have faced in this chapter leads to but one firm conviction: namely, *the Bible is the unique record of the unique Act which creates, sustains, and controls the life of the church, and is as final and unrepeatable as that Act because it is really a part of the Act. If, then, preaching is to reproduce the effects of that Act in human lives now, it can normally do this only by so rooting itself in the Bible that the Deed there recorded is transfigured into living reality now.*

The validity of this conclusion the reader must judge for himself. But if it is valid, it is both a serious indictment of our preaching and a challenge to rethink the meaning of our task in the pulpit. Have we not been too prone to determine our approach to men in the pulpit in terms of what will interest them and keep them attached to the church and bolster their moral behavior so that they shall not engage in gross sins? This approach may not be an evil in itself, but it may become so if it produces a complacent feeling of success in us and in our people and obscures the real issue of the Christian faith—a radical decision for or against Christ; not the Christ of our sentimental and romantic imaginings, nor the Christ who is the reflection of the sum total of present-day middle-class morality, but the Christ of the Cross and the Resurrection, who now sits at the right hand of God and, through his church, rules the world, and who will come again to consummate all that he has accomplished for those who "love his appearing."

For this, and nothing less than this, we must toil. And our toil must be in the Scriptures, for it was these that were "written that [men] may believe that Jesus is the Christ, the Son of God, and that believing [they] may have life in his name" (John 20:31). Our pulpits are given us to preach from the Bible. If we fulfill this high privilege, we may leave the results with God. As Suzanne de Dietrich has said:

The biblical renewal of which we speak . . . consists only in this, that the Bible is preached, taught, and received for *what it is and wishes to be:* a word of the living God alone capable of restoring man to his true destiny and revealing to him the meaning of his own history and the history of the world. Our responsibility is that this message be authentically announced. The rest is the affair of God.[26]

This is God's call to us today:

> Arise, oh, prophet, watch and hearken,
> And with my will thy soul engird,
> Roam the gray seas, the roads that darken,
> And burn men's hearts with this, my word.[27]

---

[26] *Le Renouveau Biblique* (Neuchatel: Delachaux et Niestlé, 1949), pp. 8-9.

[27] Alexander Pushkin, "The Prophet," in *Lyra Mystica,* ed. Charles Carroll Albertson (New York: The Macmillan Co., 1932), pp. 111-12.

CHAPTER III

The Preacher as Biblical Interpreter

AT first sight the Bible seems to be a divisive thing. Is it not the rock on which fellowship breaks again and again? For example, recently I saw a notice of the formation of some sort of so-called evangelical group for biblical research based on the fundamental principle of "the inerrancy of the original autographs." A former friend of mine had his name associated with this group. I immediately sat down and wrote him a letter of protest. My objection was threefold. (1) This group has no right to appropriate the word "evangelical" to their organization, for many of us are incurably evangelical who could not go with them. (2) Their platform is not evangelical, for it focuses attention not on the evangel, the "good news," but on a certain theory of inspiration. To rest on a theory rather than on God is to me just the opposite of the evangelical faith. (3) In my judgment, there is no room for the multiplication of "divisive" organizations at this critical point in world history. We would do better to get rid of some we already have. The main point at issue, however, is this—my friend and I are divided over the Bible! In this ecumenical age, then, would we not do well to shelve the Bible, or at least relegate it to a place of secondary importance, because it often becomes the source of our divisions?

I would raise a question, however, concerning this: Is this tendency to divide over the Bible the fault of the Bible, or is it not rather the reflection of our prior differences which are brought to the Bible? The Bible, along with many other things, has suffered from what someone has called "the anarchy of freedom" within Protestantism. We have not sufficiently laid aside our cherished presuppositions in coming to the Bible, but have come to it as a bulwark of defense for what we already believe. Or, in bringing our presuppositions to the Bible—for, to be honest, we must admit that it is impossible to lay them entirely aside, nor would it be wholly good if we could—they have often been theological presuppositions rather than the presuppositions of faith, creedal rather than evangelical, rational rather than religious.

The Supreme Authority of the Bible

It is surprising how much unity the Bible engenders among Christians of all confessions, *when they approach it together on its own terms.* Witness the results of the Ecumenical Study Conference held in Oxford in the summer of 1949 under the direction of the Study Department of the World Council of Churches. This group included nearly all branches of the church of Christ except the Roman branch —Orthodox, Anglican, and all brands of Protestantism. These men sat down together before a passage in Jeremiah 7:1-15, to see what agreement they could find in approaching the Scriptures on their own terms.[1] One participant spoke of the results as "amazing." The whole group gave their approval to a written statement which said: "We have found a measure of agreement that surprised us all. We submit

[1] This scriptural study, by Walther Eichrodt, appears in the April, 1950, issue of *Theology Today.*

the following statements as a general consensus." Then follow three pages of closely printed, chastely put statements of principles on which they nearly all agreed. Then note the following statements, one of which begins the first section of their report and the other of which closes it: "It is agreed that the Bible is our common starting point. . . . It is agreed that although we may differ in the manner in which tradition, reason and natural law may be used in the interpretation of Scripture, any teaching that clearly contradicts the biblical position cannot be accepted as Christian." [2] These statements suggest that to all brands of non-Roman Christianity, the Bible—if it is not the *sole* authority—is at least the *supreme* authority in Christian matters. This involves most significant agreement, a most profound sense of unity. *The Bible is our common starting point; it is our final court of appeal!*

The Bible as Instrument

Now, why is it that the Bible, which is inherently a unifying factor, so often becomes a divisive factor? In my judgment, it is because our concern is too much with *ideas about the Bible rather than with the Bible's ideas.* As long as the Bible is an object of discussion rather than a channel of communicating God's will to men, it will be a divisive thing. But when the focus of our attention is less on theories about the Bible and more on the Bible's message, it becomes a unifying factor. A group of scientists arguing about the nature of electricity might find themselves in disagreement; but if they begin to look at the objects on which the electric light falls, they will see quite alike. Or, to change the figure,

[2] See "Guiding Principles for the Interpretation of the Bible," *Interpretation,* October, 1949, pp. 457-59.

a group of people sitting before a receiving set might have wide differences of viewpoint and understanding as to the nature of radio acoustics; but if they cease their arguing, turn on the receiver, and listen, they will hear substantially the same authentic message coming from it. Even so, we must cease our arguments about the Bible and begin to emphasize the light on life that it casts.

There is a dangerous tendency in many circles today to be more concerned with what a man believes about the Bible than with whether the man believes and obeys what the Bible says. This tendency is a resurgence of first-century Judaism and is about as rigid and as fruitless as it was. Guignebert, in *The Jewish World in the Time of Jesus,* says: "The piety of Israel was measured in terms of its extreme veneration for the Law, even more than by the exactness of its observance." [3] This type of thing degenerates into more concern that a man believe in a certain theory of inspiration than that he believe he should love his neighbor as himself, or that faith, hope, and love are the only lasting and eternal values, or that in Christ, God has drawn near to men for their redemption. If, however, we concern ourselves less with theories about the Bible and more with the Bible's message and with the light it throws on life, we shall find a wide measure of agreement and harmony.

This is exactly why the study group already mentioned found unity. First, they set out to find principles of interpretation *for the use of the Bible* in relation to contemporary problems. They then sat down together before the Bible, not to assert their ideas about it, but to see what was there. And they agreed that they were jointly confronted by a Word which humbled them so that "they [were] more ready

[3] (New York: E. P. Dutton & Co., 1939), p. 64.

to listen and to discuss than they [were] to assert their own opinions."[4]

This approach suggests what might be termed the *functional approach* to scripture, or what Dr. Howard T. Kuist of Princeton Seminary has called the *instrumental* value of scripture.[5] The Bible is not an end in itself; it is a means to an end. It is an instrument through which the living God speaks to living men in the living struggle of our contemporary scene. The Bible is a catalytic agent, the instrument which produces a reaction between God and man. It is the point at which, if man listens, he hears the living God speaking to him in authentic tones which he cannot mistake for the voice of any other.

As long as the Bible is to us merely the record of what God said to men of long ago, we have failed to enter into its purpose. Or, as long as the Bible is merely a set of theological propositions, a series of rational ideas about God, it has not done its work in our lives. That leaves us still with "an unknown God," about whom we have heard but whom we have never met. When the Bible becomes not a storehouse of propositional truths, but an instrument of communication through which the living God gets at us in living relations, then and then only has it begun to do its work. Then we join with Job when, after hearing the voice of the living God, he said: "I had heard of thee by hearsay, but now mine eyes have seen thee; so I despise myself, in dust and ashes I repent" (Job 42:5-6, Moffatt).

Is not this the Bible's view of itself? Do not the Bible writers define its value in *functional* or *instrumental* terms? In II Timothy 3:15 we read of "the sacred writings which are able to instruct you for salvation through faith in Christ

[4] *Op. cit.*

[5] *These Words upon Thy Heart* (Richmond: The John Knox Press, 1947), p. 19.

Jesus." The Scriptures are *able* to do something, to function in life. And how do they do it? Not in themselves, but by confronting the soul with Jesus Christ who, through faith in him, brings salvation. Then, what of the soul who has entered this life of faith? "All scripture is inspired by God and profitable for teaching, for reproof, for correction, and for training in righteousness, that the man of God may be complete, equipped for every good work" (II Tim. 3:16-17). The function of scripture is not only to lead to salvation, but to carry the believer on to scriptural maturity manifested in ethical behavior. Paul, in Romans 15:4, states this in another way: "For whatever was written in former days was written for our instruction, that by steadfastness and by the encouragement of the scriptures we might have hope." Adding this to the former word, and summing it all up, we find that scripture's function is threefold: (1) to lead to faith in Christ; (2) to develop mature Christian character through continuous growth in this faith; and (3) to hearten, encourage, and sustain in the midst of life's discouragements. As Dr. George W. Richards has recently stated it, the "permanent value" of the Bible is the *good news* by which "we must live our lives in a world that is full of bad news." [6]

Did not Jesus confirm all this, and sum it all up, when in speaking to the Jews he said, "You search the scriptures, because you think that in them you have eternal life; and it is they that bear witness to me; yet you refuse to come to me that you may have life" (John 5:39-40)? There is no life in the Scriptures themselves. They are witnesses to Christ; they are agents to lead us to him; they are an instrument through which he may speak to us his living word. Life is in him!

[6] "The Recovery of the Bible," an unpublished manuscript.

Now on this, it seems to me, we can all agree. We may disagree on what the Bible *is*, but we can find a wide area of agreement on what the Bible *does*.

The Nature of Biblical Authority

The concomitant of this is, then, that we should approach the Bible in terms of its function, and should expect to use it for no other purpose than to find Christ and to discover the light he throws on life. To try to make the Bible yield good science, or exact history, or a literal pattern of future events, is to misuse it. The Bible is authoritative only in its own realm, as an authentic agent of the living God, whose will is the Christian's only authority. The Bible came out of history. This is its preciousness. It did not grow up in a vacuum, but is rather the record of how the living God came to meet men in living relations in history. The Bible is the record of a series of arrivals of God on the historic scene. Hence, it combines the voice of the living God and the historic scene in which that voice was heard. Thus it has the marks of history on it. And we must not confuse the human history with the voice of God. The treasure is carried in earthen vessels—we must not confuse the vessel with the treasure. The gold is imbedded in a good deal of ore—we must not mistake the ore for gold. H. H. Rowley uses the figure of "glass of various colours and opaqueness through which light passes. None of the light derives from the glass, but all is modified by the glass through which it passes." [7] Luther wrote in 1525 (what I would hardly dare say!), "The pure Scripture must be separated from its dregs and filth; which it has ever been my aim to do, that the divine truths may be looked upon in one light, and the

[7] *The Authority of the Bible* (Overdale College, Selly Oak, Birmingham, 1949), p. 11. Obviously, the glass must not be equated with the light.

trifles of these [ancient] men in another." [8] Some may object that it is difficult to distinguish between the gold and the ore. It is! But we do not solve the difficulty by trying to make the ore into gold! We do better to recognize that there is a difficulty, and to wrestle with it rather than to ignore it.

Two examples may sharpen this. In the opening chapter of the book of Exodus (verses 15-21) we read the story of the Hebrew midwives who were commanded by Pharaoh to put to death all the male children born to Hebrew mothers. They flaunted his command, and they lied to him when he upbraided them for it. Then the account says, "So God dealt well with the midwives." What, now, is the word of God in this story? Is it that it is commendable to lie if circumstances warrant it? Could one legitimately preach a sermon from this passage on the virtue of lying to the glory of God? Hardly! The question of lying is not pertinent to the passage at all. That is a matter on which we would look differently today, in the light of the full revelation of God in Christ. The falsehood is merely part of the ore in which the word of God is imbedded. The commendable thing about the behavior of the midwives is that they "feared God," and on the basis of that supreme loyalty were willing to risk their necks in violating a command of the world's most ruthless monarch of their day. Loyalty to God rather than to the state in a matter of conscience is the gold here. It must be separated from the ore of lying.

A second illustration may be drawn from the prophetic pictures of the future given in the Old Testament. In speaking of the golden age to come, the prophets were necessarily limited to the thought forms of their day. They could in no other way have made sense to those to whom they spoke. Imagine Isaiah picturing to his day the development of the

[8] *De Servo Arbitrio.* Quoted by George W. Richards, *op. cit.*

kingdom of God in the form it has assumed in the Christian church of our time! Or imagine him describing a gathering of churchmen such as our time has witnessed at Madras, or Amsterdam, or Lund! Such pictures would have meant nothing to the men of eighth-century Judah. On the other hand, it is just as foolish to insist on the literal fulfillment of the prophetic pictures in our time or any subsequent time. Dr. Albertus Pieters, in an unpublished manuscript, tells of a father who promised his young son a good horse and carriage when he came of age, if in the meantime the lad maintained the path of rectitude marked out by his father. The son made good to the father's satisfaction, and the promise had to be fulfilled. But by the time the boy had come of age, automobiles had come in. A literal fulfillment of the father's earlier promise would have been a sorry gift then! The last thing the young man wanted was a horse and buggy! The only way the father could *really* fulfill his promise was to change the form of its fulfillment from that in which it was originally given, and give his son a car. So, in regard to the prophetic pictures of the future, they were made in the forms of the day in which they were first spoken. They are fulfilled not in those terms but in forms fitting to the times of their fulfillment.

These illustrations clearly show that in seeking the word of the living God, we must go to the Scriptures not to assume that every word printed there is a divine oracle; but by utilizing our best powers to distinguish between the eternal truth and the form in which it was carried, to listen for the voice of the living God speaking to us. And we must listen for the voice of God to tell us through the Scriptures only what he designs to tell us there. He will not tell us what we can find through the microscope or telescope or in the laboratory.

The writers of the Westminster Shorter Catechism sensed this truth with regard to the Bible. In reply to the question, "What do the Scriptures principally teach?" they answer, "The Scriptures principally teach what man is to believe concerning God and what duty God requires of men." This places a proper emphasis on the function of the Bible and suggests that function to be threefold: (1) to reveal God, the living God; (2) to reveal man to himself in the light of God; and (3) to announce the "good news" that the estranged relationship between them is to be overcome by the costly redemptive action of a loving God, and that man should live in the power of this redemption (this last is an implication drawn from other teaching of the Catechism as to "what man is to believe concerning God").

When we speak of the Scriptures, then, we speak of them as a body of literature containing the record of the redemptive activity of God in history. And we believe that through that record this living God, who has supremely and permanently arrived in history in the person of Jesus Christ, speaks to us more personally and meets us more intimately than he does anywhere else. The Scriptures are authoritative, therefore, because they convey to us the voice of the living God who himself is our final authority. They are authoritative in the realm of religion only. Their authority is dynamic, not static—the authority not of the letter, but of the spirit, for as Samuel Rutherford said, "The Bible deceived the Pharisees," [9] inasmuch as they read it in the letter, not the spirit. There are many things which accompany the true revelation contained in the Bible which are not authoritative, such as slavery, polygamy, and cruelty. These are not of the essence of the revelation, but mere historic accompaniments from which the faith finally ex-

[9] Quoted by A. J. Gossip, *op. cit.*, p. 98.

tricated itself. The nature of biblical authority, therefore, lies not in every written word of scripture but in the totality of scripture as it bears witness to, and becomes the vehicle of, the living, redeeming God.

The Problem of Biblical Interpretation

I want, now, to raise a question which I cannot completely answer. How does one hear the voice of God in scripture? In what way does one determine what God is trying to say to him in his specific situation? This is no easy matter. An example will serve to sharpen the issue. A friend of mine was serving in Korea during the days when the question of shrine worship was being forced by the Japanese. A fellow missionary came to my friend and inquired, "What are you going to do about the situation—leave or stay?" My friend replied that he was not sure, but was seeking the mind of Christ in the matter. The other said, "Well, go to the Bible! That is where you find the mind of Christ! What does the Bible say? 'Occupy till I come.' It is the will of God to stay." My friend replied that he was not sure that that was the word of the Lord to him in that situation, but that he would wait for more light. Two weeks later the same fellow missionary accosted my friend again. "What are you going to do—leave or stay?" he asked. My friend replied again that he was still seeking for light. The other countered, "Well, go to the Bible! That is where you find the will of God! What does the Bible say? 'What fellowship have righteousness and iniquity? or what communion hath light with darkness?' It is the will of God to leave." Apparently God had changed his mind during the two weeks!

The Bible is an instrument through which God gets at us, but it is not an automatic thing, like a heavenly telegraph system or a divine short-wave set, on which we listen for the clicking of the keys or turn the knobs to get our answer. In fact, the word of God in one situation may be the voice of the devil in another! I do not believe this to be an extreme statement, but the sober, straightforward putting of a fact. In Isaiah's day, what was the word of Jahweh concerning Jerusalem? Was it not this: Jerusalem is inviolable! Let the world conqueror come. He can take every other city; but mighty though he is, he cannot take this city, for it is God's city. And since God is mightier than the strongest of men, Jerusalem will stand! Sennacherib is no match for Jahweh! Later on, in Jeremiah's day, what happened? Did not the people lay hold of Isaiah's sermon, which was the voice of God to his day, and utilize it in such fashion that it became the voice of the devil in their day? "The temple of Jehovah, the temple of Jehovah, the temple of Jehovah, are these," they cried (A.S.V.). Jeremiah was announcing that the city would be destroyed. No, replied the people. Jerusalem is God's city, and is therefore inviolable. God is stronger than Nebuchadnezzar! Our city will stand! *And we have scripture to prove it!* What is this but an illustration of the fact that the word of God in one historic situation had become the word of the devil in another?

More than once the difficulty of finding the mind of God through the Bible when scripture seems set against scripture was faced by Jesus. In Mark 10, when the Pharisees raised the question of the lawfulness of divorce, they quoted scripture to Jesus. Referring to Deuteronomy 24:1-4, they said, "Moses allowed a man to write a certificate of divorce, and to put her away." They had scriptural grounds for divorce, and thus could claim divine sanction for their custom. But Jesus replied to them, "For your hardness of heart he wrote you this commandment. But from the beginning of creation, 'God made them male and female.' 'For this reason a man shall leave his father and mother and be joined to his wife, and the two shall become one.' So they are no longer two but one. What therefore God has joined together, let not man put asunder" (Mark 10:5-9). What is this but an unmistakable instance of where Jesus corrected scripture by scripture? He plainly said that the passage of scripture on which they rested their case was not the voice of God to them, but a faulty concession to human weakness which ran directly counter to the true voice of God. What they took from the Bible to be a true word of God to them was in reality the word of the evil one.

But there is an illustration of the difficulty of finding the word of God in the Bible which comes much closer home to me. It is to be found in the record of the temptation of Jesus. I do not believe that in that experience the devil appeared in the form of the devil. He appeared rather in the form of holy scripture. As Jesus pondered his problem, he was faced with two strands of scripture regarding the Messiah. I believe that for long he had surmised that the Suffering Servant concept in the Second Isaiah, which nobody else accepted as messianic, was the one adequate Old Testament picture of the Messiah. At the Baptism this surmise was sealed, and Jesus set out on his public ministry to fulfill the vocation of the Suffering Servant. What then? He was driven off into the wilderness to be tempted. The Temptation was designed not so much to tempt him as to whether he were Messiah or not, but to tempt him at the point of whether he had been wrong in this new interpretation of messiahship. But the force of the temptation lay in the fact that he thought he had found this interpretation of a suffering Messiah in scripture, yet there seemed to be so much scripture on the other side of the question. Could it be that he was mistaken? Had he embarked on a wrong course,

75

to fulfill a mission which was doomed from the start? Had he found the authentic will of his Father, or had the Scriptures deceived him?

This interpretation of his struggle is brought out clearly in the scriptural background which lies behind the record of the temptation experience. Why was Jesus challenged to turn stones into bread? It was because there was Old Testament warrant for a Messiah to do just that! In Exodus 16:4 God says to Moses, "I will rain bread from heaven for you." If God did that for Moses, would he not do the same for the Messiah? Furthermore, Moses said, "Jehovah thy God will raise up unto thee a prophet from the midst of thee . . . like unto me; unto him ye shall hearken" (Deut. 18:15, A.S.V.). Did it not therefore behoove the Messiah to duplicate what Moses had done, except to exceed him in the doing of it? To prove that this was the current expectation of the Messiah, the Jews put this exact proposition squarely to Jesus. "Then what sign do you do, that we may see, and believe you? What work do you perform? Our fathers ate the manna in the wilderness; as it is written, *'He gave them bread from heaven to eat'*" (John 6:30-31, italics mine). Moses gave them bread out of heaven. If you are Messiah, you should at least do that! And they based their judgment on scripture! So, in the mind of Jesus the struggle lay in a decision between two strands of scripture. Which was the authentic voice of God to him in his situation then? That was the problem.

The scriptural basis for one of the other temptations is given. "He will give his angels charge of you," and

> On their hands they will bear you up,
> lest you strike your foot against a stone.
> (Matt. 4:6)

Again an idea suggested to his mind by scripture (Ps. 91:11-12) was warring with another idea suggested by scripture. Add to this the fact that Malachi had written, in words which practically brought the Old Testament to a close: "The Lord whom you seek will suddenly come to his temple" (Mal. 3:1). How clear it all looked! The temple was the center around which all the Jewish loyalties and messianic hopes had centered since the restoration under Cyrus. The Jews had had no independent national life, but they had a temple, and a ritual, and a law. And they were longing for a deliverance which had its emotional center there in the temple. The Scriptures had said that Messiah would come suddenly to his temple. The Scriptures also had said that guardian angels were in charge of him, who would spare him from disaster if he flung himself down dramatically in the midst of the temple. Yes, the picture fit together perfectly. And it was a picture drawn from scripture.

But there was other scripture. And the other scripture seemed to say to Jesus that the Messiah was to suffer. Out of this conflict of scripture Jesus had to find the voice of the living God to him then. His problem was: Through which of these Old Testament words is God trying to make his will known to me? And the decision was not easy! No wonder the accounts of the Temptation represent him as struggling for forty days. The struggle was not so much to do the will of God as to know it. The printed page alone did not have the answer. Through the medium of scripture, by pondering, meditating, praying, struggling, Jesus had to listen for the voice of the living God speaking to his deepest inner self.

Obedient Receptivity the Organ of Spiritual Knowledge

How did Jesus determine God's voice? What clue told him which strand of scripture was the one to be obeyed? It is very difficult to answer this. I believe, however, that there is a clue in Jesus' replies to the Tempter.

Man shall not live by bread alone,
but by every word that proceeds from the mouth of *God*.
(Matt. 4:4)

You shall not tempt *the Lord your God* (Matt. 4:7).

You shall worship *the Lord your God*
and him only shall you serve.
(Matt. 4:10)

In each of these replies there is a reference to *God,* and in two of them an explicit mention of his *lordship* over Jesus' life. Jesus' heart loyalty to God, his absolute abandonment to him and commitment to his will, became the organ by which the living God could speak to him through scripture. This is confirmed by a word of Jesus recorded in the Fourth Gospel, which I believe to be a reflection of Jesus' own experience: "If any man's will is to do his will, he shall know whether the teaching is from God" (John 7:17). It was through Jesus' willingness to obey the will of God when he discovered it that he was able to discover it. Obedience was the "organ of spiritual knowledge" for him.

In the early days of radio transmission I had a little crystal receiving set made with a pepper box and a hairpin. The hairpin served as a needle which found the sensitive spots on the galena crystal through which sound became audible. The sound was there all the time, but it could come into the range of my hearing only when the needle rested on a sensitive spot. As we approach the Bible, the voice of the living God becomes audible to us as we set the needle on the sensitive spot of obedience. Then we know the Bible to be the agent of the word of the living God not because of any a priori

78

theory of its origin, but because it has functioned in making God's voice heard. We hear by the attitude of obedient receptivity.

I am reminded of a statement in a recent article by Paul Minear, who wrote:

Those who read the gospels and who find only irrelevancies remind me of Clifton Fadiman's discussion of the reading by children of books beyond their depth. "The child reader is an automatic selecting mechanism. What he is not emotionally ready to absorb, his mental system quietly rejects." . . . As Nietzsche has written: "History will make you only those confessions which are worthy of you." [10]

For the mature reader of the Bible we might change Fadiman's statement to read: "What he is not *spiritually ready to obey,* his mental system quietly shuts out!" If we obediently approach the Scriptures, they shall function in such a vital fashion that we shall no longer need theories of inspiration to undergird them, but shall know with a certainty that lies beyond the reach of any theory that through these Scriptures the living God has met us. In a conversation Dr. Harris E. Kirk of Baltimore remarked: "I never had any theory of inspiration because I never needed any. I go to the Old Testament to find myself, and to the New Testament to find Christ, and that is all I need." The Scriptures bring us the word of God not because of any theory about them, but just because they bring us the word of God.

Dr. R. W. Dale once told of the remodeling of an English chapel. To do what was desired in changing the front of the church seemed impossible because two large pillars stood in the way. The only way the desired changes could be made

[10] "The Relevance of the Message for Our Day," *The Journal of Bible and Religion,* May, 1942, p. 89.

was to remove the pillars, and in that case obviously the roof would fall in. The problem was finally solved when an architect discovered that the pillars were "dummy" pillars which, rather than holding up the roof, were being held up by it! [11] So to many the worth of the Scriptures rests on a theory of inspiration, whereas in reality the theory of inspiration rests rather on the worth of the Scriptures. We do not believe the gospel because we believe the Bible; rather do we believe the Bible because we believe the gospel. We concur, then, with the judgment of P. T. Forsyth: "We must reduce demand as to the Bible, and press it as to the Gospel. That way lies the future." [12]

Now, what is the relation of this instrument of God's voice to the minister, apart from the fact that it is the only valid source for true preaching? I shall suggest briefly three aspects of this.

The Bible and the Minister's Own Soul

The Bible is the supreme instrument in the cultivation of the minister's own soul. Behind every sermon there must be a man, and the primary function of the Bible for the minister is to produce that man. The Bible is not for the minister chiefly a quarry of texts; it is rather the starting point from which he grows a soul. And if he is not in the process of growing a soul, his ministry is spiritually doomed before he begins. To quote P. T. Forsyth again, "The Bible is the preacher for preachers." [13] We often read the Bible to get texts to throw off on the Pharisees, or Judas, or Jonah. But this is not the purpose of the Bible. These things were "written for our learning." They mirror our own lives. We

[11] *The Living Christ and the Four Gospels* (London: Hodder & Stoughton, 1895), pp. 72-73.
[12] *Op. cit.*, p. 373.
[13] *Ibid.*, p. 17.

80

stand with the Pharisees with every attempt to attain status before men or God. The Bible's portrayal of the Pharisees is a portrait of ourselves. And Judas—who was he? He would better be forgotten if he were only an unfortunate ancient character. There is no virtue in digging up his bones to damn him again. But Judas—I am Judas!

> My weak self-will and guilty pride,
> His Judas and His Pilate were.

I am to read about Judas not to analyze his motives and describe his behavior, much less to get ideas to fill in twenty minutes on Sunday morning. I am to read about Judas first and foremost in order that through his story I may see the treachery of my own heart toward God.

The final cure for an empty professionalism is to keep close to the Bible. If we keep company with men like Isaiah, Jeremiah, Amos, and Paul, we shall be forever done with shallow impressionism in preaching which is not backed by genuine Christian manhood and wrought out in deep soul struggle. The preachers of the Bible struggled first of all with the spiritual development of their own souls. Their sermons were but the visible stains of their own life blood. We shall move in that direction as we dwell habitually in the world of the Bible.

The Bible and the Minister's Theology

The Bible is the supreme source of our theology. It will help us to avoid sentimentality on the one hand and rigid logicality on the other, by keeping our theology in living relations. All theology worth having was first of all religious experience. Its final, concrete form is nothing but a symbol to suggest the spiritual realities behind it. Our danger is that we get the symbol and miss the reality behind it. We

81

pass on the intellectual formulation without reliving the religious experience, and end in a sterile theology which is unrelated to life.

I know a man who married rather late in life. One day, prior to his marriage, he saw a lovely portrait of a girl in the studio of an art professor. He asked the professor if he could take the portrait home and hang it on his wall. Consent was granted, and the professor offered to introduce him to the girl. He demurred at that, for he said that he was afraid the living image would spoil the portrait! For four years that portrait hung on his wall. Finally, by accident he met the girl. It was love at first sight, and before long they were married. The point is this: Something happened when the two living beings met that did not happen in four years of admiring the symbol of that living being. Living relations are vital. So it is possible to admire theological symbols, creeds, doctrines, without ever coming into living relations with the God whom they seek to depict. The Bible is the cure for this. It keeps theology vital by confronting us with the living God himself.

Furthermore, the Bible helps us avoid overemphases, lack of balance, and extreme views. No doubt all theologies are in some measure based on some part of the Bible, but they do not exhaust the whole of the Bible. The Bible is bigger than any one system of thought. We must therefore avoid judging the Bible by our theologies, but must judge our theologies by the Bible. This is but another way of stating the vitalizing function of the Bible in theology, for the genius of life is proportion, and the Bible as a whole maintains our sense of proportion.

Thomas Chalmers, in speaking of the intrusion of theology into the precincts of his living relationship to his Lord,

summed up this whole question of the relation of the Bible
to theology in better words than mine:

> For the simple obedience of love which the gospel teaches me,
> I [must] either give up obedience entirely, or I find it prove
> fatiguing, because in addition to the simple feeling, I have also
> to give it its proper place in the fabric of orthodoxy, and to
> wield a most cumbersome machinery of principles and ex-
> planations along with it. Is not this scrupulous deference to . . .
> factitious orthodoxy . . . a principle altogether foreign and sub-
> sequent to the native influence of divine truth on the heart? . . .
> I look upon Catechisms and Confessions as mere landmarks
> against heresy. . . . It's putting them out of their place to look
> on them as magazines of truth. There's some of your sour
> orthodox folk just over ready to stretch the Bible to square with
> their catechism; all very well, all very needful as a landmark, but
> what I say is, do not let that wretched mutilated thing be thrown
> between me and the Bible. . . .
> Bacon compares the Bible to the well-spring and says he were
> a huge fool that would not drink but from a tank.[14]

The Bible and the Pastoral Ministry

The Bible is the prime requisite for our pastoral ministry.
There is nothing more difficult to do than to deal intimately
with people in personal relations. It is much easier to preach.
Somebody once asked Gregory of Nazianzus a question. He
replied, "I would rather answer that one in the pulpit!" It is
easier to deal with men's needs in the mass in the sacred
enclosure of the pulpit than to face them alone in the intimate relationship of a pastoral visit.

How shall this difficult task be undertaken? Without
decrying any of the value of the insights to be drawn from
the art of pastoral counseling and from the new knowledge of
the psychology of human personality that is now available,

---

[14] Quoted by James Denney in an article on Chalmers in *The British
Monthly*, September, 1904, p. 443.

I wonder if we would not do people more good by bringing to bear upon their lives some facet of truth from Holy Scripture. Alexander Whyte at times listened long to people's tales of woe without saying a word; then, with hat in hand, he would pause and quote a mighty verse of scripture and be gone. Once in taking leave of a woman suffering from an incurable disease, he quoted the Scottish paraphrase of Isaiah 40:31, "On eagles' wings they mount, they soar." Then just as he went through the door he turned and added, "Put that under your tongue and suck it like a sweetie." [15] On another occasion he sat in silence for twenty minutes while a disgruntled lady poured out her complaints. Then, arising to go, he shook hands and said, "And, mind you, forget not all his benefits." [16] Such bringing of scripture to bear on men's needs might be a more effective method of the cure of souls than much of our psychologizing.

In my own pastoral experience, two incidents of this nature stand out among others. One was that of a visit in a hospital to a patient who was in a bad condition and was uncertain of the outcome. She had come from an under-privileged background, and this illness was merely one more burden added to an already intolerable list. What could one say that would be of help? I found my word in the Bible, in Isaiah 49:16, "Behold, I have graven you on the palms of my hands." I quoted that, and said, "My sister, you are branded into the palm of God's hand. He can never hurt you without hurting himself." I know not what good it did her, but I am convinced that it was better than any word of mine.

On another occasion, my first Sunday in a country parish,

[15] G. F. Barbour, *The Life of Alexander Whyte, D.D.* (New York: George H. Doran Co., 1924), pp. 470-71.
[16] *Ibid.*, p. 365.

an elder took me to the home of a man who had been enduring a living death for months from inoperable cancer. The home was isolated and crude. The room was small, bare, crowded, filled with flies and an almost intolerable odor from the nature of the man's disease. The sufferer was in his early thirties, a husband and the father of an invalid son who was helpless and would be penniless when the father died. I scanned the room hurriedly, and on the crude dresser I saw one book—the Bible. Like a bolt out of the blue it came to me: What other book would be appropriate or adequate for this hour? I wondered even whether *Pilgrim's Progress* would have been adequate. It would have had a message. When Hopeful called back to Christian as they went through the waters of death, "Be of good cheer, my brother, I feel the bottom, and it is good," he said something which would have been of help in that hour. But, though you may think it smacks of superstition, it seemed to me that the Bible had a mightier word even than *Pilgrim's Progress* for such a time as that. "Come unto me, all ye that labour and are heavy laden, and I will give you rest." "The Lord is my shepherd." "Let not your heart be troubled." "The eternal God is thy refuge, and underneath are the everlasting arms." "I am the resurrection, and the life" (K.J.V.). Such words as these somehow become the medium through which the living Christ confronts us in all the majesty of his love in our most desperate hours, in a way that he does nowhere else.

As Henry Drummond lay dying, he asked George Adam Smith to pray and to read the New Testament. "That is the book one always comes back to," he remarked.[17] And so it is.

---

[17] George Adam Smith, *The Life of Henry Drummond* (New York: Doubleday & McClure Co., 1898), p. 501.

CHAPTER IV

The Values of Biblical Preaching

THERE is no easy answer to the problem of power in preaching. Least of all would I suggest that if one should become a biblical preacher, he would immediately become great. Great preaching has something of the mysterious about it. You can never fully analyze it nor completely account for it. In the realm of preaching that seems to be true which Jesus said of another realm, "The wind blows where it wills, and you hear the sound of it, but you do not know whence it comes or whither it goes; so it is with every one who is born of the Spirit" (John 3:8). So it is with everyone who is "born of the Spirit" to be a great preacher.

> God moves in a mysterious way
> His wonders to perform

even in preaching. It is not at all sure that the other five originally chosen deacons were either less devout or less gifted than Stephen and Philip, but there is no record, at least, of their similar effectiveness in preaching. A man may be deeply consecrated and skilled in biblical preaching, and yet get a small hearing. Dr. Marcus Dods, one of Scotland's ablest and most devout biblical students, whom Sir Robertson Nicoll called "the most Christlike man I have ever

known," [1] waited more than six years after the completion
of his studies and was rejected by more than twenty-one
churches before he received a call to a pastorate.[2] Some men
labor well, but it is not given them to reap. They may be
personally devout, richly gifted, hard students of the Bible,
and skilled expositors of its truth, and yet find themselves
crying out, "Is it nothing to you, all you who pass by?"
(Lam. 1:12.)

Other things being equal, however, I am convinced that a
man will do a greater, a deeper, a more enduring work
through true biblical preaching than through any other type.
This is supremely true because of the fact, stated earlier in
the book, that the re-enactment of the Deed of redemption
is most likely to occur when the effort to accomplish it is
rooted and grounded in the Book which is the record of
that Deed. That fact alone is sufficient to tip the scales in
favor of biblical preaching. But there are other values,
closely related to this one and in some instances direct outgrowths from it, which place the Bible in the forefront as the
minister's source of sermonic materials.

Offers Ready Supply of Sermon Material

One of the basic values of the use of the Bible in preaching
is that it gives the minister *something to preach*. And this is
no mean value! To be under the necessity of preparing two
sermons a week, in addition to some sort of midweek address,
is a demand which taxes the capacity of any normal man to
the utmost. And even should the minister be required to
preach but once a week, to stand before the same group of

---

[1] T. H. Darlow, *William Robertson Nicoll, Life and Letters* (London:
Hodder & Stoughton, 1925), p. 206.

[2] Cf. G. F. Barbour, *op. cit.*, p. 109. Cf. also *Early Letters of Marcus
Dods, D.D.*, edited by his son, Marcus Dods, M.A. (London: Hodder &
Stoughton, 1910), p. 312.

people with something worth while to say nearly fifty times a year is a herculean task. Any minister, unless he be a genius, feels the burden of this, and for many it often becomes a nightmare.

Dr. Jowett, in his Yale Lectures, tells of "one minister who, as he walked home from his church on Sunday nights, would almost invariably say to a deacon, who accompanied him, and say it with shaking head and melancholy tones, 'Two more wanted! Two more!' " [3] Another prominent minister confessed to Dr. R. Ames Montgomery, when asked how he got his themes, "That is the hardest task of all. I often spend five days in the week looking for a theme." [4]

The reason that so many men are plagued with this problem of what to preach is that they have failed to spend their study hours in the rich fields of the Bible and have gone on a vain search through the less fertile areas of mere human thought. This often furnishes rather slim picking for a full homiletic diet, and the minister finds his stock of sermonic resources growing more and more depleted.

How different the case with men who root their preaching constantly in the soil of the Bible! There is for them no dearth of ideas, no mad scrambling for themes, no sense of being pursued by the demon of next Sunday's demand. The expositional use of the Bible furnishes the preacher with an unfailing and illimitable source of sermon material. With the exhaustless mine of the Bible at his disposal, he need not either grow panicky because the week ends find him without subjects for his Sunday sermons, nor grow stale and discouraged because the subjects which he chooses fail

[3] *The Preacher, His Life and Work* (New York: George H. Doran Co., 1912), p. 121.

[4] R. Ames Montgomery, *Expository Preaching* (New York: Fleming H. Revell Co., 1939), p. 51.

to strike fire to his own soul or kindle any sparks of divine life in the hearts of his hearers. Instead of a bankruptcy of subjects and a dearth of thought, the preacher trained in the homiletical mastery of his Bible finds its pages bristling with a superabundance of pointed, practical topics for preaching and an almost extravagant wealth of "thoughts that breathe and words that burn" to develop these themes.

Give a Bible to the man who knows how to use it, plus the basic tools necessary for the study of it, and no occasion will find him wanting for a sermon theme or the material to develop it. In an unbelievable, almost talismanic way, this treasure of sermon material, instead of decreasing and being consumed, increases with use, and, like the widow's cruse, multiplies itself as it is drawn upon. To search the Scriptures has this result, says Dr. Jowett: "Texts will clamor for recognition, and your only trouble will be to find time to give them notice. The year will seem altogether too short to deal with the waiting procession and to exhibit their wealth. Yes, you will be embarrassed with your riches instead of with your poverty." [5]

Lest this should seem to be overdrawn, let us call in Charles E. Jefferson as a witness. In the Introduction to his book *The Character of Paul*, he writes: "This is a book of sermons, although the sermons have never been preached. I find that my mind, as I grow older, can create more sermons than it is possible for me to preach." [6] How did Jefferson amass this sermonic overflow? He gives us the secret a little further on in his Introduction. He writes:

For thirteen years of my life I made it my practice each succeeding year to carry away with me for the summer one of [Paul's] letters and make it my special study. Through my vacation

[5] *Op. cit.*, p. 121.
[6] (New York: The Macmillan Co., 1923), p. *v*. Used by permission of the author's son.

months he was my daily companion. I read the letter again and again. I read everything of value on the letter which I could find, meditated on its contents, pondered the problems it suggested, communed with the spirit of the man who wrote it, prepared a sermon on it, and finally made out a list of a hundred questions for the assistance of my people in their study of it through the following year. In this way Paul became to me more and more a living man. I feel I know him better than I know any other man who ever lived.[7]

What Jefferson thus did with each of the Letters of Paul he did likewise with Jeremiah, Isaiah, and other portions of the Bible, so that through a long ministry to one congregation he never ran out of rich themes on which to preach and never faced the prospect of running dry.

Robert Murray McCheyne was once asked whether he wasn't afraid of running short of sermon materials. He replied: "No, I am just an interpreter of Scripture in my sermons, and when the Bible runs dry, then I shall." Alexander Whyte, at the ripe old age of eighty-one, told a conference of ministers in Edinburgh that he never read a portion of scripture alone or at family worship but that texts "leaped out" at him as though they had been written expressly for him, and although his pulpit days were over, he selected "the most homecoming of these texts" and wrote upon it every forenoon for his "own paramount and pressing use." [8] One of Spurgeon's biographers claims for him that he never repeated himself in over 3,500 separate printed sermons, and Spurgeon himself said: "There are hundreds of texts in the Bible which remain like virgin summits, whereon the foot of the preacher has never stood. . . . After thirty-five

[7] *Ibid.*
[8] G. F. Barbour, *op. cit.*, p. 590.

years I find that the quarry of Holy Scripture is inexhaustible, I seem hardly to have begun to labor in it!" [9] Compare
this with Newell Dwight Hillis, a famous topical preacher,
who was said to have painfully repeated himself every two
years! [10] We need not belabor the point by calling in a long
line of other witnesses who could easily be summoned. It
is universal experience that men who turn to the Bible
with seriousness of purpose and a valid method of approach
to it find it an inexhaustible mine of sermonic treasures. The
giving out of truth in expositional form seems to grow
while it is dispensed. It is something which is "in diffusion
ever more intense."

Fosters Breadth of Scope in Preaching

Another value of biblical preaching is that it fosters
breadth of scope in preaching and sustains a balance and
the wholeness of a many-sided awareness of truth in one's
pulpit work. The Bible keeps our vision broad. It enlarges
our interests. It widens our appreciation of truth. It expands
our spiritual sympathies. Human nature is prone to narrowness, to onesidedness. It is easy to fall into a rut, which
has been described as "a grave with both ends knocked out."
We tend to settle so deeply into theological ruts that their
walls narrow our vision and keep us from seeing but a small
fragment of the skies of God's truth. When this narrowing
process has done its deadly work, we are inclined to put
every truth at the mercy of our pet hobby, and like Watts's
famous picture of "Hope" strum on only one theological
string for the simple reason that there is only one string left.

Jeff Ray, in his book *Expository Preaching*, refers to a

[9] Richard Ellsworth Day, *The Shadow of the Broad Brim* (Philadelphia:
The Judson Press, 1934), pp. 137-38.
[10] *Ibid.*

minister of an unnamed denomination who always got around to the subject of baptism, no matter from what text he began. On one occasion he preached from the first chapter of Genesis on the story of creation. He finally got around to the fact that God, in creating the earth, had covered about three fourths of the earth's surface with water. Since water bulked so largely in the mind of God, it was, therefore, most surely the divine intention that all men should be baptized! [11] I once knew a minister who was an ardent advocate of the doctrine of the "second blessing," who invariably arrived at some phase of that doctrine from whatever text he began. He once preached on the raising of the son of the widow of Nain, in Luke 7, from the text, "Young man, I say to you, arise," and ended up on the "second blessing"! These are undoubtedly extreme illustrations which overemphasize the tendency we are bringing into focus. But they suggest a danger to which we all, in lesser degree and in less obvious ways, frequently succumb. Dr. Kenneth Foreman some years ago recalled the argument between two ladies who were praising the merits of their respective ministers. Said one, "Our minister is wonderful. He can preach a dozen sermons from the same text." The other replied, "Our minister is more wonderful still. He can take any text in the Bible and preach the same sermon from it!" [12] One fears that this champion of her minister's excellence is not so far wrong as we would like her to have been!

The danger of neglecting certain phases of truth and over-emphasizing others is a real one, and one which may warp and disfigure both the thought and character of those who are victims of it. The cure for this is so to root one's preaching in the total sweep of the biblical revelation that

[11] (Grand Rapids: Zondervan Publishing House, 1940), pp. 104-5.
[12] "A Pew Considers the Pulpit," *Union Seminary Review,* January, 1940, p. 127.

the sanity and balance of the Bible itself are reflected in the resulting sermons. No true understanding of God's Word, nor a proper portrayal or adequate appreciation of the character of the God there revealed, can be reached by a hit-or-miss, hop-scotch type of preaching. Only as one comes to understand and to use the Bible as a unified whole, and to see each of its parts in relation to the rest of it, can he acceptably interpret God to men and lead them into a type of Christian experience which is at once deep and broad, which has its roots inextricably entwined in the rich soil of unshakable conviction, yet raises its broad branches high into the clear skies of Christian sanity and rationality, and bears the fruits of understanding and true tolerance.

Much of the appalling ignorance of the most elementary foundations of our faith and the moral and spiritual futility which characterizes a great deal of our present-day Christianity arise from homiletic feeding which has all the weaknesses of an unbalanced diet. Some preachers feed their listeners on a diet composed largely of theological pepper and vinegar which produces conviction but is accompanied by unpleasant religious prickly heat and lacks the clear, rosy complexion of normal, healthy Christianity. Others present a constant menu of desserts and side dishes which are tasty and temporarily exhilarating, but tend to eventuate in a soft, flabby religiousness which has little or no spiritual muscle and bone, and produce a moral drowsiness that is deadening. Still others overload their listeners with the heavy staples of Christianity, the stick-to-the-ribs foods, which build up muscle and supply energy, but do not provide sufficient opportunity for them to work off their reserve of energy through the proper exercise of putting the Christian graces into daily practice, and thus produce men who are morally and spiritually muscle-bound and awkward.

This distortion of Christian wholeness goes hand in hand with a distorted understanding of the character of God, which results from a failure to root our preaching about God in the broad sweep of the total biblical revelation. Our sermons are frequently cartoons which caricature rather than characterize the God we worship. We take our partial ideas to a text for sanction, rather than letting our thoughts be expanded and corrected by a larger grasp of God born out of a continuing study of the total body of Holy Scripture. How patient God is with our distorted portraits! Sometimes he seems to be all nose, with his chief purpose that of sniffing heresy and condemning it. At times he is all head, an intellectual concept. At other times he is all heart, the sum total of human sentimentality and grandfatherly indulgence. At still other times he is all hands, working continually in his creation, but having no ears to hear his children speak to him, and no time for, nor interest in, pausing to speak with them and to have intimate fellowship when heart beats with heart and the language of love is spoken. Such caricaturing is open to the criticism made by Carlyle of one of Burns's biographers, that he errs "in presenting us with a detached catalogue of his several supposed attributes . . . instead of a delineation of the resulting character as a living unity." [13] The "several supposed attributes" of the God of our faith must be combined into a "living unity" before men can view him with true appreciation and understanding, and intelligently and devotedly offer their lives to him as instruments of accomplishing his will in the world.

This character of God "as a living unity" cannot be known by chance acquaintance on special occasions, but must be sought in the continuous unfolding of his nature throughout

[13] *Carlyle's Essay on Burns with Poems from Burns,* ed. William C. Gore (New York: The Macmillan Co., 1931), p. 3.

the entire course of his dealings with men in living relations. He must be seen under all aspects and observed under all conditions. He must be known in his loves and in his hatreds; in his tenderness and his severity; in his joys and his disappointments; in his chastenings and his rewardings; in his changelessness and his tractability; in his power and in his amazing restraint; in his dealings with primitive men and with men more matured and developed; in his mode of revealing himself to men of all races, classes, and conditions. And these different views must not be permitted to flit before the mind in a disconnected, rapidly changing, kaleidoscopic way which would confuse and distort; but they must all be seen as integral parts in a long-developing divine drama, each stage of which without the others could "not be made perfect." We must pray with George Herbert:

> Oh that I knew how all thy lights combine,
> And the configurations of their glory!
> Seeing not only how each verse doth shine,
> But all the constellations of the story.[14]

It is this sense of wholeness which a truly Bible-centered ministry alone can foster.

Herein lies the hope of the ecumenical movement, for it is the wholeness of the Bible which saves from sectarianism. The narrowness which usually characterizes sectarianism results from two basic causes. First, many of our peculiar differences are the outgrowth of an overemphasis arising out of some historic situation. The exaggerations of partial truth growing out of the pressures of conflict often become anachronistic after the passing of time. Sectarianism is the insistence on the permanent validity of the scars of conflict

[14] "The Holy Scriptures," in *The Poetical Works of Herbert and Vaughan* (Boston: Houghton Mifflin Co., 1880), p. 62.

as of the essence of truth. For this the Bible is the corrective. It was not born in one historic situation, but was fifteen hundred years in the making. The external structure of its faith changed from time to time, but the central core of revelation remained the same. Whatever the peculiarities of the historic situation, men were always confronted with the same God coming to them both in judgment and in grace, calling forth the same response of trustful commitment. Through this means peripheral matters separated themselves from the central issues of the faith, so that the Bible, as the time-tested witness to the revelation, becomes the final guide for each generation in its quest for truth. It sets over against the narrow particularity of one historic moment the universality of a broad sweep of history, and aids us in sifting the essence of eternal truth from the specific forms in which that truth was cast in any age.

The second root of sectarianism is the failure to understand the many-sidedness of truth, and to identify our own partial grasp with the whole of truth. In facing an octagonal object, for instance, I can see one side plainly and two sides obliquely, but there are five sides which I cannot see at all. They are nonetheless parts of the total object just as much as the three sides which are visible to me. Should I insist that the three sides I see are the whole of the object, I should be both partial and false. This is what happens when we identify some sectarian emphasis in religion with the whole of truth. The Body of Christ becomes divided, and a competitive spirit replaces the sense of unity which ought to prevail among Christians. The remedy for this, however, is not for anyone to deny the truth which he sees plainly, and to reduce our understanding of the Christian faith to the lowest common denominator of that on which we can all agree. That would leave us little if anything to believe and would be suicide for the faith. How much better would it be for us to share what we see and see plainly! This is a process of mutual enrichment of the faith instead of mutual surrender of conviction and impoverishment of the faith, and this process adds to each phase of truth which one sees clearly other phases of truth which others see clearly. In this alone lies the value of the ecumenical movement. And it is the Bible which serves as both stimulus and guide to this process. It depicts the spiritual experiences of many men, from all walks of life, with all types of personality, from varied historic situations, faced with a complexity of problems—all confronted with the same God, all responding to him in their way. To root one's preaching in the whole of the Bible, therefore, is one of the best means of delivering one from a narrow presentation of truth, and forces him into ranges of truth to which he would otherwise be blinded.

Dr. Jowett, a man who was singularly delivered from the partial apprehensions of truth to which many men give vent in the pulpit, tells us that for long years he followed the practice of looking at truth through other men's eyes. He said:

> I ask how would Newman regard this subject? How would Spurgeon approach it? How would Dale deal with it? By what road would Bushnell come up to it? Where would Maclaren take his stand to look at it? Where would Alexander Whyte lay hold of it? . . . I have looked at the theme through many windows, and some things appear which I should never have seen had I confined myself to the windows of my own mind and heart.[15]

I am convinced that this breadth of view on Dr. Jowett's part was fostered, partly at least, through his close fellowship with the Scriptures. He was a thorough and ardent student of the Bible and considered it his task in the pulpit

---

[15] *Op. cit.,* pp. 127-28.

to set forth its meaning in forms intelligible to those to whom he preached. This constant soaking in the Scriptures led him, by a process of gradual absorption, to acquire something of their catholicity of spirit. What was true for him may well be true for others. Bible-saturated preaching produces breadth without shallowness.

Stresses Abiding Realities

Still another value of preaching from the Bible lies in the fact that it will keep us dwelling upon the great abiding realities of our faith rather than on the transient fancies of the moment. The Bible forces on one the necessity of preaching on the central eternal verities, giving short shrift to the shifting currents of modern thought which pass with the setting of the sun. Preaching ought to be related to modern thought, surely, but it ought to interpret the eternal truth of God to the modern mind and enforce the abiding realities which remain true for all time. The ancient Archimedes once said that he could move the world if he had a lever long enough and a place on which to stand. Much modern preaching has a long lever, but no place on which to stand. If preaching is to have the power to move the modern world, it will have to have its feet planted not on the world itself, where they merely press harder and imbed more deeply the very thing they are trying to move, but on the firm, immovable bedrock of eternal certainty.

If it were not pathetic, it would be amusing to scan lists of sermon subjects which one often sees. Too many of them reflect P. T. Forsyth's scornful description of sermons "in which the week's events supply the text and the Bible only an opening quotation." [16] Dr. Jowett once described a preacher as a visible newspaper "editor, presenting his message amid

---

[16] *Op. cit.,* p. 9.

the solemn inspirations of prayer and praise." [17] A newscast, or a sociological treatise, or a half hour of humorous entertainment with ethical overtones, sanctified by being offered in God's house, is not Christian preaching.

I sat through a preaching mission in a large city for most of a week some years ago, where leading ministers from all over America addressed daily and nightly audiences of from two to four thousand people. To me, the week was one of the most tragic I have ever witnessed. There was much enthusiasm, much eloquent oratory, much plying of the stock-in-trade which is supposed to influence large crowds, much humor—but with the exception of two sermons, nothing that I heard had the remotest relation to the great central themes of our faith. Grace, justification by faith, forgiveness, the atonement, the Incarnation, the deity of Jesus, the meaning of the Resurrection—one could have listened all week and never have discovered that these great verities had any relation to the Christian faith whatsoever. The whole thing was superficial, trivial, false. It was contemporaneous, but not eternal. It offered men no firm place on which to stand secure amidst the swirling currents of modern confusion. The listeners did not hear, through the voice of man, the voice of God sounding above the madding roar of this world's turmoil. The gospel presented did not "rise above the spirit of the age and . . . enter into the spirit of all ages and speak her language." It could well have fallen under the censorship of Dean Inge when he said, "If you marry the spirit of your own generation you will be a widow in the next. . . . The votaries of progress mistake the flowing tide for the river of eternity, and when the tide turns they are likely to be left stranded like the corks

[17] *Op. cit.*, p. 90.

and scraps of seaweed which mark the high-water line." [18]

A word from the late Percy Ainsworth, of Britain, very aptly expresses the point under consideration.

> Perhaps the Church is too much at home in the world. We talk much about meeting men on their own ground, about understanding the spirit of our age, about keeping abreast of the times. Within certain very narrow limits there is truth in these phrases; but there is not in all of them put together, and in all kindred pleas and policies, one atom of the truth that saves the world. . . . It is not this world we need to know better, it is the other world. It is not the language of the street we need to master, it is the language of the kingdom where He reigns whose voice has the music and throb of many waters. . . . The sick and the dying, the heartbroken and the desperate, the burdened and oppressed, will find nothing in our easy up-to-dateness to encourage them to trust us with one shamefast confession, one spiritual difficulty, one precious secret of hope or fear or sorrow.
> It is to the stranger in the earth that the fore-wandering souls of men instinctively turn.[19]

So much of our preaching is full of human trivialities which in the long run do not matter very much. We hear people remark about preachers, "Isn't he cute!"—as though the function of the pulpit were to offer "cute" entertainment to help while away Sunday for churchgoers! I know a minister to whose wife the worst remark I ever heard about a sermon was made. "Tell your husband," said a lady to her, "that his sermon was just darling!" There was something of spiritual reality lacking either in the sermon or in the woman! In any case, even though the lack may have been more in the woman than in the sermon, the minister went home to repent, and to vow before God that he would forever do his best to avoid preaching "darling" sermons. The Bible does

[18] *Diary of a Dean* (London: Hutchinson & Co., Ltd., 1949), pp. 12, 198.
[19] *The Pilgrim Church* (London: Robert Culley, 1910), pp. 19-21.

100

1946?

not deal on such superficial levels. With it as the chief source
of our preaching, we shall find ourselves digging around the
roots of great concepts, of eternal realities, which shall abide
"the war of elements, the wreck of matter, the crash of
worlds."

The Bible is the cure for pulpit trifling. To wrestle with
its message is to be delivered from paltry themes which, however interesting, do not anchor men to the Infinite when
the guy ropes of time stretch and strain and snap. To roam
through the Bible for one's sermons is to find truths which
call from out the deep of the Eternal's heart to the deep
of our confused and frantic world. The Bible enables us to
appraise the present moment against the backdrop of God's
forever. Said Alexander Whyte, in a letter to a fellow minister:

Somehow, unaccountably, a great gospel text is always the
most difficult text to me to preach on, so as to make it fresh and
interesting. But, difficult or easy, I must preach more on such
texts. And so must you. It is for such texts, above all else, that we
have our pulpits committed to us. . . . Did you ever grapple with
"the Blood of God"? I am to try that soon.[20]

It is by mastering the content and the spirit of the Scriptures, and assaulting the souls of our hearers with the tremendous truths with which the Bible is alive, that we shall
be able to undergird them "for the facing of this hour." We
live in a day when slight cures are of little avail. Calamity
has brought its full strength to focus on human life "to knead,
overturn, and trample it, to squeeze blood and tears from
it, to twist it like a whirlwind, to storm it like a tempest, to
consume it like a flame." Men need to be confronted with
that eternal kingdom which "cannot be shaken," and summoned to enter it. It is the realities of that kingdom with

[20] G. F. Barbour, *op. cit.*, p. 308.

101

which the Bible deals, and true biblical preaching will set against the transient fancies of this world the grand and heartening wonders of the "age to come."

Glorifies Offensive Themes

A further gain of biblical preaching is that it sometimes enables the minister to dwell inoffensively on some themes which might cause offense if they were attacked directly or topically, rather than growing out of an exposition of scripture. Brastow says of Robertson of Brighton, "He availed himself of the expository method, as a wise homiletic and pastoral device, in getting difficult and offensive themes before his congregation." [21] This device of Robertson's will stand a modern minister in good stead. In a day when the church has been invaded by secular standards of conduct and ethical norms which are quite unrelated to the gospel, a faithful minister finds himself under the necessity of raising issues against which the natural man sets himself in revolt. Little good is to be done if dealing with these hard issues should degenerate into a contest of minds between the minister and his people. If, however, in the natural course of unfolding the meaning of various passages of scripture from the pulpit these unpleasant questions inevitably open up simply because the Bible has something to say about them, then the offense becomes the offense of the Bible and not that of the minister.

More than once when I have been taken to task, following a sermon, by someone who disagreed with what I said, I have found it a happy device to agree with my accuser that I did not like what I said any better than he did, for it was as hard on me as it was on him and cut as sharply across my

[21] *Representative Modern Preachers* (New York: The Macmillan Co., 1904), p. 71.

own human judgment as it had his; but I was not giving out my own ideas from the pulpit, but declaring the word of God as I understood it in the Bible. If, therefore, my critic did not agree with what I had said, and could show me that I had misinterpreted the Bible, I would readily concede the point. But if that were not the case, there was no quarrel between him and me. Rather the quarrel was between him and the Bible. And if the hearer did not like what God had said through the Bible, he should take him to task for it, not me! And it is not impossible that once the issue is thus shifted to the truth of the Bible, so that the contest is no longer between man and man, but between man and God, the resentful critic might come to grips with the deeper issue involved and ultimately respond to the truth which at the moment he so bitterly resents. Henry Ward Beecher once remarked, "There are many topics which, from the excitement of the times and from the prejudice of the people, it would be difficult to discuss topically in the pulpit, yet, taken in the order in which they are found in Sacred Writ, they can be handled with profit, and without danger." Then he added that even "the squire can hardly stamp out of church for a 'Thus saith the Lord.' " [22]

This expository approach to difficult themes has the psychological advantage of surprise attack, of getting people's defenses down, so that one can score heavily when the "punch" really comes. It has the value of gaining the assent of the mind and will to a proposition or a truth or a principle before any application is made. Then, having attained that assent, it is a more difficult thing for the hearer to wriggle out of the clutches of the truth when the application is made. This is an old and effective device. Nathan secured David's

[22] *Yale Lectures on Preaching*, First Series (Boston: The Pilgrim Press, 1904), p. 225. Used by permission.

assent to a principle, then suddenly pointed the accusing finger, crying out, "You are the man!" Amos secured the approval of his audience on the general theme that the sinful behavior of their neighbors demanded God's judgment before he concluded that their own behavior made a like demand. Jesus used the same method with Simon the Pharisee and with the lawyer to whom he spoke the parable of the Good Samaritan. The Bible bristles with living situations which make spiritual principles clear. To set these forth in expositional form and then to thrust them home to the contemporary scene is the likeliest way of making real inroads on the sins of modern men.

Acquaints People with Scriptures

Another value of biblical preaching is that it may become a teaching device to help acquaint with the Scriptures the people to whom one preaches. The Protestant Reformation was rooted in the conviction that the faith of the church could maintain its vitality only as the common believers fed their daily lives on the resources of the Bible. Consequently, Luther translated the Bible into the common language of the man in the street and preached from the Scriptures in a fashion designed to send his hearers back to a study of the Bible itself. He said on one occasion, "I should prefer all my books to perish that only the Bible might be read." [23]

The appalling ignorance of the barest content of the Bible, to say nothing of its deeper meanings, on the part of the laity today is not a question of mild humor but a cause of grave concern. For as surely as time gets its revenges, Romanism, out of which Protestantism was born, will reap a harvest—is reaping a harvest—out of this failure of Protes-

[23] *A Compend of Luther's Theology*, ed. Hugh Thompson Kerr, Jr. (Philadelphia: The Westminster Press, 1943), p. 16.

tantism to be true to her own genius. To survive, a movement which was born in the matrix of the Bible must be nourished on that which gave it birth.

Preaching from the Bible serves the dual purpose of instructing people in the Scriptures through the very act of preaching and of stimulating their own inquiry into the Bible as well. Long and fruitful ministries have again and again demonstrated the effectiveness of biblical preaching in this regard. Dale's biographer, in commenting on a series of expository sermons he preached at Carr's Lane Chapel, remarked that "the congregation was like one great Bible Class: there was a Bible open in almost every hand." [24] Dr. James Palmer, who was associated with Dale's successor, Dr. Jowett, after he had come to the Fifth Avenue Presbyterian Church in New York, once told a group of students that Jowett's preaching had exactly this same effect. As he preached, there were dozens of people throughout the congregation, Bible in hand, following through the scripture passage as the sermon progressed. And one can be very sure that many of those who found the service of worship a time of opening up the Scriptures were stimulated to some real searching of the Scriptures on their own part during the days between services.

Times have changed, of course, and it is not as likely that people will carry a Bible to church as it was in the days of Dale and Jowett. Nor would I suggest that one is to measure the success of a man's ministry by the number of people leafing through the Bible as he preaches. But most people today who do not carry a Bible under their arm to church do not carry it in their heads either. And they are doomed to a continuing biblical illiteracy unless the brief moments they

[24] A. W. W. Dale, *Life of R. W. Dale of Birmingham* (London: Hodder & Stoughton, 1898), p. 111.

spend in church become occasions when the treasures of the Bible are unlocked for them, and they are made to see something of the Bible's relevance to our day and the power of its message to transform life. This cannot be done by preaching which is conceived in the head of the preacher, then has a biblical text attached to it at the last moment as a sort of springboard from which to launch into the preacher's own thought, or as a sort of fetish to give divine sanction to a man's words. A recovery of understanding the Bible on the part of the laity is dependent on preaching which begins, continues, and ends with the Bible—preaching whose theme, structure, elaboration, atmosphere, and goal are all direct outgrowths of the passage of scripture on which one is preaching, and which is normally undergirded by illustrations drawn from the full range of biblical truth.

The minister who does not sense this is missing his greatest opportunity, and, if the definition of preaching set forth earlier in this work is valid, is also recreant to his duty. No man has a right to stand in a Christian pulpit and pretend to speak the word of life to men without first brooding over the pages of the Bible until the word of the Lord comes to him through it, so that what he says is a fresh announcement of the witness of scripture to Jesus Christ. When this is done, however, those who come to worship, if they listen at all, automatically get some beginnings at least of an understanding of the scripture passage on which the sermon is based. And under the impact of a continued pulpit ministry of this type, direct study of the Bible is encouraged which, on the part of the spiritual nucleus of the congregation, will eventuate in the strengthening of faith and a deepening of Christian devotion and loyalty.

Henry Ward Beecher bore witness to this in telling of

an eminent pastor in Ohio, who, probably, never in his life preached any other sermon than an expository one. The Bible in his hands, Sunday after Sunday, was his only sermon. During a long pastorate, he went through the Book from beginning to end, and often, and the fruit of his ministry justified his method. It was proverbial that no people were more thoroughly furnished with knowledge, with habits of discrimination in thought, or were more rich in spiritual feeling.[25]

This proved true, too, in a more recent ministry, that of the late Charles E. Jefferson. It was Jefferson's custom to make out lists of thought-provoking questions on areas of scripture on which he was preaching, and have them mimeographed for his people to encourage and guide them in their own personal study of the Bible. And the method bore fruit, as his long and effective ministry testified.

Perhaps one of the most worth-while things to be accomplished today by a pulpit ministry rich in biblical truth is that it helps to ground one's people in such a fashion that they are not so easily tossed about with every wind of doctrine which blows in their direction. Promoters of religious fads are wise enough to gain a hearing always by claiming to base their supposed insights on the Bible. They are not, of course, rooted in the Bible at all, but are rather stuck into biblical soil without growing there. Anyone thoroughly acquainted with the Bible would recognize them for what they are, and with one thrust would push them over and disclose the fact that they had no real rootage in scripture truth. But what of the layman untutored in his Bible? He is often fooled by appearances and captivated by certain bizarre or eccentric features which by their very strangeness seem to him to have some supernatural quality which brands them as religious. When once he has made the leap and attached him-

[25] *Op. cit.,* p. 226. Used by permission.

self to one cult or another, it is then usually too late to rescue him, for any attempt to expose the nonbiblical basis of his new-found credulity is repulsed by a mind too fettered for free thought.

The remedy for this is so to acquaint people with the Scriptures before they are captivated by the half-truths of modern cults that they shall know what to make of them when they appear. This will demand an educational program in the church which is broader than the preaching hour, but this educational effort should be oriented around the preaching of the gospel from which it takes its meaning. And the minister can have no more vital part in it than making his sermons occasions when the grandeur of the gospel lays hold of men's lives, and the Deed of redemption is made so vital that men shall be led into an ever-growing inquiry into the record of that Deed. The Bible in the pulpit is both the safeguard against error and the granary of spiritual food for the souls of one's people.

Imparts Authority

The final value to be dealt with is that the use of the Bible gives one a sense of authority in his preaching, a sense of being backed by the whole weight of the Hebrew-Christian tradition. There is a sense in which it is utterly presumptuous for a man to stand before other men and announce to them eternal truth. And the way it is frequently done is indeed presumptuous! What right has one man to tell another man what to believe? By virtue of what inherent authority can a man, himself caught in the coils of sin in which we are all entwined, himself desperate, bleeding, and broken, offer advice to other men as to how to overcome their spiritual ills? This is indeed the final presumption, an audacity that becomes insolence if we only knew it. When, in pulpit after

108

pulpit across the land, frail men have the brashness to offer their paltry thoughts and shabby counsel to other men in the name of God, it is little wonder that the world does not stop to listen nor to take the Christian faith seriously. Their ideas are as good as ours. Their guesses have as much claim to truth as ours. And why not?

If we had the Christian grace to see ourselves realistically, many of us would shrink from ourselves in disgust because of the unspeakable bumptiousness with which we have stood in Christian pulpits assuming an authority over people's minds and hearts which we do not have, and trying to force down their throats morsels of our own weak wisdom as the bread of life. When we stand behind a pulpit and face a congregation, what is our task? To give out our own poor ideas? No! We have no word of our own for the ills of the world in this dread hour. When we speak a word of our own, we are at best healing the hurt of the world slightly, if at all. Unless our message is an unfolding of the meaning of the Scriptures, we are orators and not preachers. And the world will never be saved by oratory—only by God!

The only authority any man has to stand before other men and proclaim spiritual truth is that he should at that moment be the agent of God, to whom alone belong "the kingdom, and the power, and the glory." And to be the agent of God's authority is to bear witness to what God has done for men in Christ, as this is recorded in the Bible and experienced by men who have believed it in all ages. "When you have the preacher's Bible," said Henry Ward Beecher, "you have that which is like a living power, and you are a trumpet, and the life of God is behind you, so that the words which come from you are breathed by him." [26] The preacher's thought is not to be his own thought, no matter how rich his mind. He does

[26] *Op. cit.*, Third Series, p. 59.

not create truth; he bears witness to truth. Whatever fresh-ness he has is not to be the freshness of novelty but the fresh-ness of insight into what the church has always believed. He does not initiate new truth, but appropriates old truth. His spontaneity is not to be the discovery of that which others never knew, but rather the "spontaneity of power" in appro-priating and enforcing the revelation made by God in Christ —a revelation already full, final, and complete, always believed by the Church universal. It is not the minister's business to say a new thing, but to say an old thing with new power. Great artists are not those whose originality consists in creating something new, something sensational, but those who give an original setting to the old realities of nature, who help other men see what is already there. They do not create; they appropriate, then communicate to others. Gainsborough, for example, did his work without what men call "originality." He kept within the limits of the time-tested principles of art and portrayed through his own genius his personal discovery of what was already "given" in nature. At the same time there was a painter named Fuseli, "who used to eat raw pork for supper, slept on it, and the next day painted what he had seen." His work was original! He was not painting old things in his own new way, but was paint-ing new things. A few years ago "there was a sale of pictures, and one of Gainsborough's paintings was offered. It had no 'originality,' but it was received with a cheer, and fetched eight thousand pounds. The very next picture put up was by Fuseli—and it fetched a guinea!" [27] The world soon tires of "new" things.

When a man preaches, if he knows what Christian preach-

[27] From an unpublished series of lectures delivered by Dr. Sedgewick at the Lutheran Theological Seminary, Gettysburg, Pa., in the spring of 1938.

ing is, he is but bearing witness to the holy, catholic, apostolic faith "once for all delivered to the saints." This faith was not born with him, and it will not die with him. It is the permanent heritage of the faithful. His preaching, then, is the church's preaching. He merely becomes in that historic moment the mouthpiece whereby the faith of the church founded on the apostles and prophets expresses itself.[28] "If you want to be an original preacher," said R. W. Dale, "look at heaven and hell, life and death, sin and holiness, with your own eyes; listen for yourselves to the voice of God; ask Him to reveal to you the glory of His love, the steadfastness of His truth, the energy of His righteousness, and tell the world what you have heard and seen." [29]

Obviously, the old faith needs new applications and new interpretations to meet the ever-changing needs of human life in successive generations. But the gospel being interpreted and applied is not new, nor does it ever change. It is the authoritative voice of the Church universal, whose authority is that of its Lord who created it and by whose grace it continually lives. The minister's authority, then, is the authority of Christ which is not conferred upon him by any occult mystery, but by virtue of his membership in Christ's Body. As the Body speaks forth the thoughts and feelings of the Head, it bears the Head's authority. If it severs itself from the Head, its authority is immediately extinct. But how may the Body be assured that it is in living touch with its Head and thus bearing his authority? Only through the Bible, which is the record of the creation of the Body and the instrument of its constant renewal. The Head, who is "the same yesterday and today and forever" can only speak

[28] In this judgment I am deeply indebted to P. T. Forsyth, especially for his chapter "The Preacher and His Church; or Preaching as Worship," in *Positive Preaching and the Modern Mind.*

[29] *Op. cit.*, p. 297.

now what he spoke then. His living voice is but the renewal of the living voice of the past, and it comes to us through the record of that voice in Holy Scripture.

Preaching which severs itself, therefore, from the Bible can have little or no valid authority over men's minds or hearts, for it is an irreverent assumption of authority which no living man may rightly claim. Our mission is to bring to the Scriptures all the resources we can muster from linguistic, exegetical, historical, and literary study; then to ponder, meditate, pray, and be gripped by what God is trying to say to our generation through the passage with which we are dealing, then present that to our people. This gives us the backing of the whole Hebrew-Christian tradition, and the authority of the truth by which the Scriptures have survived the ages. The faith is not ours. It is God's. And he has revealed himself to us in Christ. And it is through the Bible that Christ meets us supremely. The only right we have to preach is to preach Christ as he makes himself known through the Scriptures of the Old and New Testament. "The Lord has yet more light and truth to break forth from His written Word," said John Robinson as he sent the Pilgrim Fathers off from Holland to America. "More light and truth." But where? *From His Written Word!*"

In a memorable passage in *Pilgrim's Progress,* Great-heart comes upon Mr. Valiant-for-truth, who has just won a great battle. "Then said Great-heart to Mr. Valiant-for-truth, Thou hast worthily behaved thyself. Let me see thy sword. So he showed it him. When he had taken it in his hand, and looked thereon a while, he said, Ha! it is a right Jerusalem blade." Then Mr. Valiant-for-truth replied, "It is so. Let a man have one of these blades, with a hand to wield it and skill to use it, and he may venture upon an angel with it." The word of God revealed through the Bible is that sword.

112

CHAPTER V

The Implications of Biblical Preaching

THE concept of preaching set forth in the former chapters carries with it certain inescapable implications. Basic issues are determinative of broad relations. Whether unconsciously or consciously, one's understanding of the essence of his work mightily affects the prosecution of his task at every level. Almost every phase of a minister's work bears some relation to his appraisal of the central meaning of preaching. If preaching is rightly understood as the point at which the whole history of redemption is brought to a contemporary focus in the life of both preacher and congregation, then certain other things follow as the night the day. It is to these that we now turn our attention.

Preaching and Success

One clear implication is that this view of preaching delivers ministers from false standards of success. Since the Church, whose life is in the realities that are unseen and eternal, must of necessity exist in the seen and the temporal, it is always tempted to appraise its achievements by measurements that are largely secular. Ask a minister how his work is going, and, if he is happy in his work, all too often will come the reply: "Excellently! We have added 250 members during the past nine months. Our budget has increased 22

113

per cent during the current year. Some influential families, recently moved to the community, have joined our church. The annual bazaar was a grand success. We have resurrected the men's organization and added two members to the staff." And so the account goes on.

Now, inasmuch as the Church must embody her spiritual values in visible, organizational, concrete form, it would be folly to hint that such gains as these mentioned, and many others like them, are to be totally discounted in measuring the effectiveness of a church's witness. But it is quite possible for a church to be effective in these visible areas without doing the distinctive work of the kingdom of God in the slightest. The budget, membership, attendance, and interest of the Rotary Club or a carnival or a professional baseball club may also be on the increase. But that is not necessarily an indication that the spiritual values of the community are rising. There is likewise no inevitable relation between the outward progress of a given church and its spiritual index. It is difficult to measure faith, hope, and love. Statistics can never quite capture heart loyalties. Devotion, the struggle after holiness, self-discipline, prayer, the agony of yearning with Christ over the waywardness of a broken world and the abandon with which men walk in darkness when they could walk in the light—these are not to be entered on church records.

The fallacy of measuring spiritual success by visible conditions may be one into which Americans peculiarly fall, but it is by no means a monopoly of theirs. In the days of the pre-exilic prophets the outward prosperity of the religious structure of the nation became a liability, blinding the people to the real lack of spiritual vitality in the nation. And when the prophets denounced them as essentially irreligious, the people stood aghast and pointed to the flourishing visible

114

signs of religion as final evidence of spiritual health. There was once a church, too, which surveyed its status with complacent confidence, saying, "I am rich, I have prospered, and I need nothing." It was a rather rude thrust for the apostolic writer to reply, voicing the judgment of the risen Christ, "[You do not know] that you are wretched, pitiable, poor, blind, and naked" (Rev. 3:17). And we forget that it was not a wayward individual but a prosperous Christian church which kept Christ standing outside the door. It was to men most sure of their spiritual status to whom the poignant word of the risen Christ came, "Behold, I stand at the door and knock; if any one hears my voice and opens the door, I will come in to him and eat with him, and he with me" (Rev. 3:20).

A true awareness of the meaning of preaching is a good antidote to this fallacious equating of secular status and spiritual success. A man who knows that he is called to be the saving agent of God's redemptive purpose will hardly be lulled into a feeling of success by the plaudits of the public or the empty approval of ecclesiastical courts. Success? Who dares claim success as an ambassador of the Almighty? When one has given his best, all he can do is to "bow [his] forehead to the dust, and veil [his] eyes for shame," and own that he is an "unprofitable servant."

Some years ago, while visiting in the home of a minister of a medium-large, influential Protestant church, I asked him how his work was going. He replied that his membership had increased; his budget had enlarged; his people were kind to him, having given him a good manse, a worthy salary, a car, and a great deal of personal affection. "But," said he, "when all is said and done, I cannot see that I am really accomplishing very much for the kingdom of God." He then went on to specify that he lived in an area of special social tensions which his church was not only unwilling to help alleviate but fostered; that his people were worldly and self-indulgent; that the secular tone of life stuck out at every point through the thin religious veneer; that causes for which he had labored incessantly were opposed by the economic interests controlled by his officers; and that his leading members advised him—in all good will—not to get so bothered about the issues which he believed to be vital to the kingdom of God, because there was little use to be concerned over things about which one can do nothing. (And, may I hasten to add, he was not a member of a fringe group, nor an ultraconservative in theology, nor a pessimistic crank. He was a large-souled man, of broad sympathies, who held the respect of the whole city in which he lived, among members of all denominations and those of none, to a degree that I have seldom seen equalled.) As I talked with him, something within me rejoiced, and I said to myself, "Here is a man who knows what he is called to do, and has not succumbed to the ordinary standards by which men measure ministerial success." With a man at the helm who could not be lulled into complacency by outward success and personal laurels, there seemed to me to be some hope that God might break through the crust of middle-class respectability that passed for Christianity in that city and do a vital redemptive work.

If preaching is the actualization of redemption through the miracle of grace as the living Lord himself confronts worshiping men through the word of the preacher, one can never fully know to what degree he has succeeded in his ministry. It is impossible for men to see as God sees, who looks not on "the outward appearance" but on "the heart." Hence, one may have succeeded in the very moment when to all appearances he is a total failure. On the other hand, he may have failed utterly when every outward indication points to success. The minister who, under God, was the agent of Wendell Phillips' conversion, never knew it—never discovered that at the conclusion of his sermon the young Phillips went to his room, knelt alone, and gave himself to his Lord. Conversely, many a minister has been bent under the weight of congregational compliments at the conclusion of his sermon, whose work may have been "wood, hay, stubble," bearing no lasting fruit whatsoever for the kingdom of God.

To understand the meaning of preaching rightly is to be delivered both from unworthy pride in any supposed success and from equally unworthy despair at any seeming failures. To preach as redemptive event is to cease searching for visible signs of response, and to abandon once and forever observable results as the motivation of one's ministry. It is to do what Alexander Whyte advised his nephew to do, when he said, "From the time you enter the pulpit think of nobody: neither yourself . . . nor anybody else. When you give out your text . . . say with Newman: 'May the motive of the preacher be the salvation of the hearer, and may the hearer's motive be his own salvation.' " [1] This shunning of overt norms by which to judge success, and this concentration on the re-enactment of redemption, whether it is manifest to the preacher or not, is what keeps one going when there seems to be no outward sign of success. This is what enabled Adoniram Judson, after years of toil and suffering in Burma without success, in reply to a question, "Do you think the prospects bright for the speedy conversion of the heathen?" to answer, "As bright as the promises of God." [2] This is the cure both for ministerial pompousness and for

[1] G. F. Barbour, *op. cit.*, pp. 470-71.
[2] Stacy R. Warburton, *Eastward! The Story of Adoniram Judson* (New York: Round Table Press, 1937), p. 70.

"blue Mondays." "When the Lord comes," said Paul, "He will bring into the light of day all that at present is hidden in darkness, and He will expose the secret motives of men's hearts. Then shall God Himself give each man his share of praise" (I Cor. 4:5, Phillips). Not what succeeds now, by the standards of a secular world, but what will be seen as success then, is all that really matters. In the meantime the minister's chief concern is "that he should prove worthy of his trust" (I Cor. 4:2, Phillips).

Preaching and Worship

Another corollary of preaching as redemptive event is that it delivers from a false cleavage between the sermon and the "worship service" and places the sermon squarely at the center of the whole worship experience as the core and kernel of it all. One of the reasons for the decline of preaching in our time has been the movement toward the "enrichment of worship," fostered by what Dean Inge called as early as 1927 "a few 'liturgiologists' who took their pseudo-science very seriously." [3] The justification for this has been that the Puritan strain in Protestantism tended to denude both churches and worship services of the aids which beauty and symbolism can offer. Furthermore, it has been argued, the central position of the sermon in traditional Protestant services tended to exalt the preacher too much, substituting instruction and exhortation for true worship and making the preacher focal in the service instead of God.

Let it be admitted that there is some truth in these accusations. Man is a sensory being, and the proper use of the eye and the ear may be a valid aid to worship. It is true also that preachers are notoriously self-centered creatures, with the natural human trait of placing oneself at the center of

[3] *Op. cit.*, p. 126.

the universe (since everything we apprehend must of necessity be apprehended from the position from which we view it) abetted by the fact that their position automatically places them at the center of most occasions. But one fears that the proposed cure for this barrenness and man-centeredness of worship in the recent trend toward ritualism may be as bad or worse than the disease, and that unless it is checked before it goes too far, the last state of Protestantism will be worse than the first. To cast out the demon of barrenness with the demon of aestheticism is merely to substitute Beelzebub for Satan. And between the two there is little to choose!

It has always been true that when the vitality of true religion has waned, men have sought to fill up their spiritual emptiness with an increased attention to the mechanics of worship. The prophets never denounced the Levitical worship per se, but they saw in it again and again a façade behind which men hid from themselves their own essential irreligiousness, and a ready aesthetic and legalistic substitute for the true worship of God. Jesus never outlawed the temple worship as such, but he saw it functioning for many as a substitute for true worship, for men the more heartily went through the motions of worship as their spiritual emptiness increased. He therefore insisted that true worship was not to be identified with place or form, but was the heart's response of faith to God "in spirit and in truth." What the prophets saw in ancient Israel and what Jesus saw in first-century Judaism can be seen likewise in the history of the Christian church. Ritualism often tends to increase as spiritual religion decreases; and although it cannot be fairly denounced as an evil in itself, ritualism offers a ready means by which men whose inner vision of God has grown dim can substitute for that the deceptive emotional response to

119

aesthetic beauty. "The glacial age is now over," said P. T. Forsyth, "when religion was in peril from natural science; in our more genial day the danger is from other and sunnier sides; and one of these is the aesthetic." [4]

It is, of course, a debatable question, but one cannot help wondering whether the resurgence of ritual in our time marks not a real deepening of our spiritual life, not a real yearning after a more vital worship, but rather the last desperate effort of a decaying Protestantism to hide from itself its true condition. If men, in going to church, fail to have high dealings with the eternal God, they can at least, through an aesthetically designed ritual, have the emotions stirred and the feelings soothed and find some temporary escape both from the chaotic world and from the God who pursues them but whom they seek to elude. This resurgence of ritual may be Saul's last effort to conjure up the appearance of realities long since dead as a substitute for the obedience of the heart which has lapsed long before. Harris E. Kirk some years ago described this tendency toward "enrichment in worship" as "a colorful medievalism without God, a kind of high sacramentarian atheism." [5] Carlyle spoke of it even more sternly as "Idol-worship and Mimetic Dramaturgy, instead of God-worship," which, he added, the Puritans felt it was "very dangerous indeed for a man to have concern with." [6] These are strong words—but what if they should be true!

H. H. Farmer writes incisively of the danger to which we are calling attention when, after expressing a fear of

[4] *Christ on Parnassus* (New York and Toronto: Hodder & Stoughton, 1911), p. *ix.* Forsyth, of course, does not entirely rule out the aesthetic from religion, but insists that it must be the "servant," not the "master," of religion.

[5] *Op. cit.,* p. 171.

[6] *Oliver Cromwell's Letters and Speeches* (London: Chapman and Hall, 1870), I, 39.

music which can "so easily stimulate emotions far beyond any point to which real insight and genuine decision of will" would ever take one, he says:

I suspect that in church many a man has mistaken the oscillation of his diaphragm in harmony with a ten-foot organ pipe, or the quivering of his heart strings to the melting sweetness of a boy's voice, for a visitation of the Holy Spirit. And there are other ways of working on the emotions—ritual, vestments, the vast grandeur of Gothic cathedrals, the dim, romantic light of stained glass, the cunning artifices of modern flood lighting. And the preacher, if he have certain gifts, a hypnotic eye, a magnetic presence, a numinous voice, a solemn unction, aided perhaps, as I have once or twice observed, by a darkened building and one spot-light over the pulpit, can take his place in the scheme.[7]

The relation of all this to preaching is that it tends to relegate the sermon to a secondary place in the worship service, and to make men think of it as something other than worship and something less worthy than worship. The implication is that during the "worship service" the congregation does business with God, but that during the sermon they listen to another man's opinions on religion through which their own thinking is stimulated either by agreement or disagreement. And since this process is less exalted and more human than the "worship service," it is crowded more and more into the background both as to the time allotted to it and as to the importance attached to it. Again and again one is invited to preach in a service which is so elaborately designed that by the time the preacher begins, the congregation is emotionally surfeited and physically fatigued. As one looks out over the people, they look back at him with the glazed eyes of those who, as "good soldiers

[7] *The Servant of the Word* (New York: Charles Scribner's Sons, 1942), pp. 75-76. Used by permission of the publishers.

of Jesus Christ," are willing to "endure hardness" for the next twenty minutes or so, always with a teleological interest—which is another way of saying, "How long, O Lord?" or "How far away is the end?"

The cure for this is to understand that the sermon, *provided there is real preaching,* is not an adjunct to the worship service, but the heart and climax of it. It is the point up to which all else leads; it is the place where God draws nearer to the worshipers than at any other part of the service. It is the point at which God "speaks" more clearly than he can through any other means. Speech is always in the form of symbols which communicate meaning from one person to another. The effectiveness of speech, therefore, is determined by the communicative potentialities of the symbols used. God has many ways of speaking, many symbols through which he communicates with men. But since his full and final word was spoken in the Incarnation, this suggests that the human personality has more communicative potentiality than any other mode of speech which God uses. Therefore, the most effective means which God has of speaking to men now is through the medium of human personalities.

If preaching is what we have here tried to set forth—the redemptive activity of God focusing in a mighty conflict with human souls through the activity of the preacher, then the divine activity can operate more potently through the act of preaching than through any other means. The God who incarnated himself in the historic events of Calvary and Easter, now reincarnates himself in the activity of the preacher to actualize for "these persons here present" the Deed wrought in history so long ago. This is clearly set forth in Dr. Gossip's description of the conception of the sermon in the Reformed service.

The preacher has come out from the hush and secret of the Presence, where for a week he has been listening and brooding, face to face with God in a silence other men cannot attain, and where the divine voice can carry clearly. And now he is speaking to us in God's name, and standing in Christ's stead, bringing a message straight from very God to very us, which, partly at least, we can really catch through the stumbling and stuttering of the man seeking to express and share it with us. That is the meaning of the ministry: why men are set apart. That is the purpose of the service. God is here; is taking action upon our behalf; has come with grace for us. Down on your face, and worship! [8]

This conception of preaching means, then, that the sermon, rather than being a side issue, or an appendage to the worship service, is the point to which hymns, prayers, scripture, responses, all lead; the point at which the God who speaks through all the elements of the worship service makes himself known in a clearer, more decisive way than at any other point of the service. "It is not God's ordinary way," said John Donne, "to be whispering of secrets. For Publication of Himselfe He hath constituted a Church. And in this Church . . . His Ordinance of preaching batters the soule, and by that breach, the Spirit enters; His Ministers are an Earthquake, and shake an earthly soule; they are the sonnes of thunder, and scatter a cloudy conscience." [9] The living presence of the Redeemer himself, speaking through a redeemed man announcing the redemption to others who listen and respond in faith, is the final realization of Christ's word, "Where two or three are gathered in my name, there am I in the midst" (Matt. 18:20). If both preacher and people understand what preaching is to be, the

[8] *In the Secret Place of the Most High* (New York: Charles Scribner's Sons, 1947), p. 122. Used by permission of the publishers.
[9] Quoted by James Stewart, *Heralds of God* (London: Hodder & Stoughton, 1948), p. 211.

123

sermon can never be crowded out for time, nor looked upon as a human discussion of religious questions or a discipline which must be endured, but it will always be the point to which they look forward week by week as the most meaningful factor in sustaining the soul's relation to God.

Preaching and the Sacraments

A further concomitant of this view of preaching is that it is a corrective for sacramentarianism, which is a growing peril of Protestantism. Sacramentarianism may be defined as the exaltation of the sacraments to a position of inherent worth apart from the preaching of the Word—the tendency to impart to baptism and the eucharist some magical spiritual efficacy in themselves. This is evidenced by an increasing tendency on the part of Protestant churches to rally their people to attendance once every three months for the administration of the Lord's Supper, as though there were some special value to be received merely by being present to partake of the elements of bread and wine, whether one gathers regularly in the fellowship of the people of God or not. This seems to be coming dangerously close to Ignatius' "medicine of immortality" view of the sacraments.[10] Further evidence of this trend toward sacramentarianism is the increasing substitution of an altar for the communion table, the removing it from the level of the people and placing it above and beyond them in the chancel, and the accompanying shift of emphasis toward the minister as priest. I recently saw a new chapel of a traditionally free-church denomination where a large stone altar had been set high in the chancel with an iron rail around it, as

[10] *Eph.* 20. Quoted by J. H. Srawley, "Eucharist (to end of Middle Ages)," *Encyclopaedia of Religion and Ethics,* ed. James Hastings (New York: Charles Scribner's Sons, 1924), V, 547.

though the holy of holies into which we enter by the blood of Jesus were again available to men only through the mediation of an official priesthood. One cannot sit in judgment on individual churches or denominations to whom such things are precious. But it would not seem unfitting to raise a protesting voice against a trend which, if universally adopted, would revert to a medievalism and a mimicry of Romanism which are alien to the genius of Protestantism and from which we were delivered by the blood of men who died for better things.

I am not pleading for a low view of the sacraments. It is no doubt true that the Puritan strain in Protestantism has left many of us with a truncated understanding of their worth and their place in the New Testament scheme of things. But I am suggesting that the evils which led our too severe forefathers to extreme views were real, and that they are realities no less dangerous to us today. And the path toward restoring the sacraments to their rightful place in Protestantism is not by a new exaltation of ceremony and mechanics but by a new and profound understanding of their meaning. P. T. Forsyth said:

All worship, however Protestant, must have some ritual. . . . The question of a little more ritual or a little less is a small one. A greater question is what is *meant* by the ritual, be it less or more. Is it the ritual of a minister or of a priest? That is the point. . . . To have a minister at all is to have a ritual. The real question is as to the place of ritual, small or great, in salvation. Does salvation depend on the acts done either by the congregation or in its name—upon sacraments? [11]

The only priest we can now have, in the New Testament sense, is Jesus, "who is seated at the right hand of the

[11] *Christian Perfection* (London: Hodder & Stoughton, 1899), pp. 88-89.

throne of the Majesty in heaven" (Heb. 8:1); the only altar we can have is not an altar "made with hands" but an unseen altar in "the inner shrine behind the curtain, where Jesus has gone as a forerunner on our behalf . . . into heaven itself" (Heb. 6:19-20, 9:24). And the sacramental symbols which dramatize these unseen realities can be saved from superstition, sentimentalism, and vapid aestheticism only as they function in the context of the dynamic witness to the invisible realities which lie behind them through preaching.

I have recently seen Calvin called in as a witness to the fact that the Protestant Reformers were much more sacramentarian than their later Puritan followers, and to undergird a plea for a deeper emphasis on the sacraments in worship today. It is no doubt historically sound that Calvin himself felt that the sacrament of the Lord's Supper should be observed in the gathered fellowship of the congregation each Lord's Day, and that he accepted the less frequent observance of it as a compromise with the Geneva fathers. But it is to be remembered that Calvin never valued the sacraments apart from their relation to preaching, and it is doubtful whether he would approve the sacramentarian trend now which seems, as it increases, to cause preaching to decrease. In commenting on Acts 10:37, where Luke speaks of "the baptism which John preached," Calvin wrote:

We must note the phrase, that John preached baptism. For Luke comprehendeth, indeed, under the word *baptism*, all the whole ministry of John; nevertheless he showeth that it was no dumb sign, and void of doctrine. And assuredly this is the chiefest thing in all sacraments, that the Word of God may appear engraven there, and that the clear voice may sound. For which cause, that wicked profanation which is seen in Papistry is so much the more to be detested, because, *burying preaching*,[12] they do only charm the sacraments with magical enchantment.

It is clear from this that Calvin sanctioned no observance of the sacraments which buried preaching, and that he abhorred, as the importation of magic into religion, any view that divine grace was imparted through the sacraments apart from faith which was born and quickened by the activity of God through the work of preaching. I think Calvin would have agreed heartily with Forsyth's statement that "nothing but the Word made Sacrament can make a Sacrament out of elements, and keep it in its proper place." [13]

In a recent work by Phythian-Adams a distinction is made between the minister as an *agent* of God and the minister as an *instrument* of God, the distinction being that an agent of another acts for the other through the functioning of his own personality whereas an instrument is a passive medium, inertly responding to the will of the one using it.[14] This distinction serves to sharpen the issue here being discussed. The sacerdotalist tends to feel that the sacraments somehow impart divine grace through being distributed by the priest, apart from the functioning of his own personality at all. It is doubtful, however, if God ever degrades a human representative to the role of a mere instrument. Would it not be more correct to suggest that the bread and wine are instruments—inert symbols of deeper realities—and that the minister is always an active agent of God? The efficacy of his administering the elements lies not in the physical act of distributing them—that is a mere mechanical necessity— but in the spiritual act of preaching, announcing the realities of which the elements are signs. The true administration

[12] Italics mine.
[13] *Op. cit.*, p. 85.
[14] *The Way of At-One-Ment* (London: SCM Press, 1945), pp. 89-95.

of the sacraments lies in the preacher's being used of God to make real, in the act of preaching, the death and resurrection of Christ in the heart of the believer. It is not, of course, argued that this must be true each time the believer partakes of the sacrament, for one could well partake of Christ through the elements of bread and wine in true faith, even though this were not immediately accompanied by true preaching. But specific occasions always move in the broad context of a believer's total experience, and previous encounters with the living God through the announcement of his Word must always lie in the background to make the believer aware of what is happening in the sacrament—or nothing happens. Only as the believer participates in the sacraments with the faith born of preaching, do the sacraments really do their work. H. H. Rowley has remarked that Paul was an ambassador, not a postman.[15] It may well be said that ministers are personal agents of God, not mere errand boys delivering God's grace as inert instruments.

There was a true symbolism in the simple Protestant churches in which many of us were reared. A communion table—not an altar—was set on the floor level, symbolizing the gathered fellowship of the worshiping family of God around the table of their Father. The broken body and shed blood of Christ were not magic elements to be distributed by an ecclesiastical official, but signs that all present were united by the events of Calvary and Easter as members, through faith, of the Body of Christ, the fellowship of the redeemed. Above the communion table stood the pulpit, with an open Bible, and behind that the preacher, the living agent of God's redemptive Word. As the minister announced God's redemptive Deed recorded in the Book, faith was

[15] *The Relevance of the Bible* (New York: The Macmillan Co., 1944), p. 47.

born in the worshipers, and the sacrament became the external sign which proclaimed the Lord's death and witnessed to the fact that those who partook were members of the fellowship of his Body, living in love, working in faith, with the patience of hope, until he brings his kingdom to a consummation. This is symbolism, New Testament symbolism, and rightly relates preaching to the sacraments, without which they ultimately degenerate, as Calvin insisted, charmed "with magical enchantment."

Preaching and the Congregation

Another truth which follows from the conception of preaching here set forth is that true preaching is not only a function of the preacher, but of the congregation as well. The Deed of redemption is actualized as the worshipers respond to the approach of God to them through the word of the preacher, so that both God's self-giving and man's receiving are essential parts of the total process of preaching. Consequently, if the worshipers fail to realize what is supposed to happen through a sermon, and listen either listlessly or faithlessly, they can make it almost impossible for a minister to preach in the deepest sense. Preaching is not the function of an individual, but of the church. It is to the church that Christ's presence is promised. "For where two or three are gathered in my name, there am I in the midst of them" (Matt. 18:20). The very word "church" involves a "called out" group, called out of the world into a fellowship of faith. The New Testament figures for the church are corporate—stones built into a temple, priests in a priesthood, citizens of a holy nation, brothers in a family of faith, members of a body, partakers of a koinonia, a fellowship.

It has been strongly urged of late that the Church exists only when a congregation is gathered in the name of Christ

to worship.[16] This is not the place to debate theoretically
whether the Church exists even when men are not gathered
for worship. But the whole debate is focusing increasing
attention on the fact that the church is not merely a collec-
tion of religious individuals, but a corporate Body, and that
a religious gathering can be said to be the Church only as
men realize that they are gathered in the name of Christ, that
they are mutually members of his Body by faith, and that
they find their relationship to him complete only in the
mystic unity of the entire group.

It is this capacity of the fellowship of believing men to
release the redemptive power of Christ which lay behind
Paul's insistence that the worship of the Corinthians should
be conducted with decorum and intelligence. For, said he,
"if all prophesy, and an unbeliever or outsider enters, he is
convicted by all, he is called to account by all, the secrets
of his heart are disclosed; and so, falling on his face, he
will worship God and declare that God is really among you"
(I Cor. 14:24-25). This passage suggests that when an unbeliever enters a Christian gathering, he should be brought
within the sphere of unseen lines of spiritual force which
vitalize the entire group and influence him in a way that is
not possible in any mere individual encounter.

Sienkiewicz catches this truth when in his *Quo Vadis?* he
pictures a young Roman, Vinicius, who, in love with a beautiful Christian girl who has spurned his love because he is
pagan and has fled from him, goes in search of her to a
secret night gathering of Christians for worship in the
Ostrianum, a Roman cemetery. Sitting there incognito, a
pagan in a Christian worship service, he hears Peter preach

[16] Cf. Karl Barth, "The Church—The Living Congregation of the Living
Lord Jesus Christ," *The Universal Church in God's Design* (New York:
Harper & Bros., 1948), pp. 67-76.
130

and is caught up into the sphere of spiritual influence created by the response of the group to the preaching. How does this affect him? "He felt," says the writer, "that if he wished . . . to follow that teaching, he would have to place on a burning pile all his thoughts, habits, and character, his whole nature up to that moment, burn them into ashes, and then fill himself with a life altogether different, and an entirely new soul." [17] That is what preaching is designed to do, and would do far more often in our day if the conditions for doing it were created by the preaching of the minister and the response of the gathered congregation.

This conception of the vital part played by the congregation in a worship service lies behind the exhortation of the writer of the Epistle to the Hebrews that his readers must not neglect "to meet together" (Heb. 10:25). The writer truly sensed that nothing could take the place of the gathered fellowship of the people of God, and that to neglect corporate worship was not only to cut oneself off from the potent spiritual influences of corporate worship, but was also to let the whole group down by not being present to contribute one's part to the total good.

The final reinforcement of this is to be seen in the symbolism of the eucharist, where men eat together as a family at the table of the Lord and partake of his redemptive benefits not as individuals but only as members of his family. The Protestant doctrine of the priesthood of believers has frequently been warped by well-meaning but mistaken champions of individualism in religion to mean that each man is his own priest before God in a solitary way. In the New Testament, however, one is a priest himself only by virtue of his incorporation into a "kingdom of priests." [18]

[17] (New York: Grosset & Dunlap, 1925), pp. 130-31.

[18] Cf. "Many Members," by Samuel W. Newell, Jr., *Interpretation*, October, 1951, pp. 425-26.

The rights of the individual are valid only in the fellowship of the Brotherhood. Protestantism stands for *personal* faith, but not for *individual* faith. And there is a great difference!

This means, therefore, that to recover great preaching we must rediscover that preaching is the mutual function of minister and people. Unbelievers will normally respond in faith to the redemption set forth in preaching when the congregation of believers responds in faith anew and actually becomes the Body of Christ, the reincarnation of the presence of the Redeemer himself. The secrets of men's hearts will be disclosed, and they will declare that God is really present, when that is actually true. But if the professed believers do not respond to the preaching in faith, then God is not actually present any more than he is in any other gathering of men, and the Deed of redemption is not actualized. The greatest of preachers have realized the impossibility of really preaching without the response of the congregation. Henry Van Dyke at times stopped his congregation in the middle of a hymn and called out, "If you people won't sing, I can't preach!" He meant something deeper than that he missed the note of human enthusiasm which he needed to buoy up his own spirit. He sensed in the dull singing a lack of awareness on the part of the people of the tremendousness of the gospel about which they were singing; and he knew that unless they rallied their own devotion to Christ, it would be utterly impossible for him to proclaim the evangel with effectiveness.

A. J. Gossip, when he was just beginning his ministry, was taking Sunday evening tea with Alexander Whyte. Whyte asked why Gossip had not been at the services that day, and Gossip replied, "I was taking duty in a certain church."

"Where were you?" inquired Whyte. Upon learning where, he questioned, "And how did you get on?"

"I found it cold," replied Gossip.

"Cold!" exclaimed Whyte. "I preached there two years ago, and I have not got the chill out of my bones yet!" [19] If any man had both the native gifts and the spiritual power to move men, it was Alexander Whyte. But he knew perfectly well that a congregation unresponsive to the gospel made it absolutely impossible for him really to preach. Someone has said that the great preaching of Scotland in the heyday of the Scottish pulpit was the result of the Scottish congregations as much as of the preachers. If a sacred writer could remark that even Jesus "could do no mighty work there, . . . because of their unbelief" (Mark 6:5-6), it may with equal cogency be said of many a preacher, "He could do no mighty preaching there because of their lack of response."

Kierkegaard once pointed this truth in a remarkable illustration drawn from the theater.

It is so on the stage, as you know well enough, that someone sits and prompts by whispers; he is the inconspicuous one, he is, and wishes to be overlooked. But then there is another, he strides out prominently, he draws every eye to himself. For that reason he has been given his name, that is: actor. . . . Alas, in regard to things spiritual, the foolishness of many is this, that they in the secular sense look upon the speaker as an actor, and the listeners as theatergoers who are to pass judgment upon the artist. But the speaker is not the actor—not in the remotest sense. No, the speaker is the prompter. . . . The stage is eternity, and the listener . . . stands before God during the talk. . . . The speaker whispers the word to the listeners. . . . The listener's repetition of it is what is aimed at. . . . God is the critical theatergoer, who

[19] Barbour, *op. cit.*, p. 138.

133

looks on to see how the lines are spoken and how they are listened to. . . . The speaker is then the prompter, and the listener stands openly before God. The listener . . . is the actor, who in all truth acts before God.[20]

If this be so, a recovery of great preaching is at least partially dependent on congregations. If men stagger into the house of worship on the Lord's Day bleary-eyed from a late "binge" on Saturday night, having lived through a secular week in which God was very far from their thoughts, with no spiritual preparation of their hearts for worship and with little understanding that they are gathered in the fellowship of the saints to actualize once more on the contemporary scene the redemptive power of the Cross and the Resurrection, there is little likelihood that much great preaching will be done. It is difficult to bring to birth the Deed of redemption in the sterile womb of a secular church.

We ministers ought not to excuse ourselves too lightly for our failures, laying them at the door of the congregation instead of at our own door. But at the same time, if we are to restore preaching to its rightful place in Protestantism, we must not only recapture for ourselves its meaning, but must try to instruct our congregations to that end and plead with them to join us in an effort to glorify the work of preaching. Robert E. Speer once remarked that in his judgment Horace Bushnell was the greatest preacher in the English language. But he hastened to add that if Bushnell were here today, he would find it difficult to get the average American congregation to respond to his preaching. Perhaps more of us will have to follow in Bushnell's train, grappling with great biblical truths in a profound way, then seeking

[20] *Purity of Heart.* tr. Douglas V. Steere (New York: Harper and Bros., 1938), pp. 163-64. Used by permission. I am indebted to my colleague, Prof. Balmer H. Kelly, for calling my attention to this remarkable statement.

to train congregations who can "take" that sort of preaching, before the pulpit will regain its power over Protestantism.

Two concomitants of this should be mentioned. One is that radio and television preaching can never replace the gathered fellowship of Christians to hear and respond to the living voice of God through the living voice of a preacher. Perhaps for shut-ins or those employed during worship hours, who cannot meet with God's people yet sense the spiritual bonds which unite them with the larger fellowship, the radio or television may afford a true means of worship. Perhaps, too, there are many individuals who are really led to Christ by means of the gospel announced over the air. But one thing is sure, the reality of the faith of those thus converted is questionable if they do not soon attach themselves to some congregation of the Body of Christ. And if all men should forsake the assembling of themselves together and habitually listen to radio services in their homes, the church would soon die.

The other suggestion is that going forth to coax into church membership people who have not been attending its services and hearing the message of redemption has great dangers of superficiality and spiritual futility. I have myself, with guilty conscience, participated in visitation efforts which simply padded the rolls of the church and enlarged the already massive supply of "dead wood." I have ignominiously witnessed, too, instances where those who were "signed up" for membership in the church could not be got out to a worship service to be publicly welcomed into the fellowship which they had allegedly entered. One wonders whether the method might be changed in the direction of inviting people to come to the house of God to be instructed in the Christian faith, hear the word of God proclaimed, and then make their decision either for or against their Redeemer. There are few groups into which one may be inducted with as little knowledge of what is involved as the average modern Protestant church. It would be well to have people show their interest in "joining the church" by attending the services of the church for a period, listening to the announcement of redemption, and understanding some of the implications of their faith for life before they make their final decision. It is common practice on many mission fields to require a probationary period of six months to a year in which a candidate for church membership is given opportunity to demonstrate the depth of his commitment before he is received as a communicant member. If such practice is out of the question here, it might at least caution us against an overreadiness to take people into the church without a more determined effort to get them to see the meaning and the implications of the step they are taking.

Another remark of Kierkegaard's is in point here. "For long the tactics have been," said he, "to use every means to move as many as you can—to move everybody if possible—to enter Christianity. Do not be too curious whether what they enter *is* Christianity. My tactics have been, with God's help, to use every means to make it clear what the demand of Christianity really is—if not one entered it." [21] This statement may be overdrawn, and in a measure may set up a false antithesis, but it contains enough truth to bear repeating and to foster caution. Men are not usually so easily converted that it is consummated in a brief unannounced appeal to sign up for membership in the church. Unless they acquire some grasp of the meaning of their redemption and become vital, working members of the fellowship of faith, the reality of their religious conversion is suspect.

[21] Quoted by P. T. Forsyth, *The Work of Christ* (New York and London: Hodder & Stoughton, 1910), p. *ix.*

Preaching and Teaching

What we have been saying raises the question of the relation of preaching to teaching. This question is somewhat difficult to deal with, because the distinction between these two words in modern parlance differs from their distinction in the New Testament sense. The modern distinction is a difference of *method*, whereas in the New Testament the difference is one of *content*. To preach was to announce the facts of the gospel; to teach was to set forth the ethical implications of those facts. Hence, to utilize a modern pedagogical method rather than the didactic method to set forth the facts of the gospel would, in the New Testament sense, be as worthy as preaching inasmuch as it is an announcement of the facts of redemption. On the other hand, to try to teach religion merely by drawing out the religious opinions of the students, without confronting them with the facts of God's redemption, could hardly be classed as a Christian procedure, nor could it in any way be the equivalent of preaching in the sense set forth here.

A "gospel" is a proclamation, something to be announced, something to be offered to men. If the facts of the announcement are introduced by indirect pedagogical means, one cannot quarrel with this method so long as the announcement finally penetrates the consciousness of the student. But when the teaching of religion becomes not just a pedagogical method of acquainting students with the gospel, but substitutes the religious thoughts of man for the announcement of the basic gospel data, it is likely to be a futile process from the standpoint of producing true Christian faith. Teaching that is concerned with "what man may believe" more than with "what God has done for man" is less than Christian.

It is doubtful whether teaching of this sort can ever produce Christian faith. Unless men are confronted by the redeemer God through the announcement of the gospel so that the Deed of redemption is consummated in their lives in a mighty regenerative act, the teaching of the gospel is "foolishness" and falls on deaf ears. John Foster tells of a lad from the Scottish highlands, where the United Free Church was referred to as the U.F., going to visit some high-church Anglican relatives in England. As a part of the process of putting him to bed, his aunt ventured on some instruction about angels. The instruction fell on deaf ears as the little boy simply replied, "We don't make much of angels in the U.F." [22] Likewise, modern man does not make much of a good many things which are essential to the Christian faith, and unless the redemptive power of the gospel transforms men's inner lives, Christian teaching falls on deaf ears. Men must not only have the truths of religion set before them, but must have the power to understand them created. As George Florovsky has recently said, Christian doctrine "can be apprehended and understood only in the living context of faith, by which I mean in a personal communion with the personal God. Faith alone makes formulas convincing; faith alone makes formulas live. 'It seems paradoxical, yet it is the experience of all observers of spiritual things: no one profits by the Gospels unless he be first in love with Christ.' " [23] The creation of the power to grasp Christian meanings may, under God, be consummated through a teaching process, but it is more likely to be brought into being through the fellowship of men who are met to worship, whether in the home or the church, and supremely in the approach of God to men through preaching. Then, when

[22] *Op. cit.*, p. 63.
[23] "As the Truth Is in Jesus," *The Christian Century*, December 19, 1951, p. 1458.

the faculty of insight into Christian truth has been created, teaching takes its proper place in leading men, through thoughtful reflection, into a deeper understanding of their faith and an awareness of its implications for life. I once heard the biblical mind likened to Adam, who spoke only Hebrew, and the modern mind likened to Prometheus, who spoke only Greek. The plea was made that if Prometheus knows only Greek, then Adam had better learn to speak Greek if he wants to get his truth over. Within limits this is true, but it is perhaps more true that there are basic elements in the mind of Adam which are not translatable into modern thought and speech, and that if Prometheus ever wants to understand Adam, he must learn Hebrew. P. T. Forsyth, who was often criticized by others on the ground that the man in the street would not understand what he was saying, once remarked, "The truth of Christianity cannot be proved to the man in the street till he come off the street by owning its power." [24] Teaching is designed as a tool of Christian nurture, but it can function only within the context of living faith. It can never, therefore, replace preaching, which is designed to announce a gospel that brings men into living relations with the Lord of the church, so that they are ready for instruction which shall open up to them the deeper implications of the life which is now theirs.

In this connection, there is a call for further thought as to the wisdom of "junior churches." They obviously have their value, but does the gain offset the loss? Can youngsters, who are yet too immature in faith to realize the meaning of the fact that a worshiping congregation is a part of the Body of Christ gathering in fellowship with their Lord and with the saints of all ages, realize the sense of the

[24] *The Cruciality of the Cross* (London: Hodder & Stoughton, 1909), p. 4.

Divine Presence as they can in experiencing worship with adults? A word from Albert Schweitzer is pertinent here.

From the services in which I joined as a child I have taken with me into life a feeling for what is solemn, and a need for quiet and self-recollection, without which I cannot realize the meaning of my life. I cannot, therefore, support the opinion of those who would not let children take part in grown-up people's services till they to some extent understand them. The important thing is not that they shall understand, but that they shall feel something of what is serious and solemn. The fact that the child sees his elders full of devotion, and has to feel something of their devotion himself, that is what gives the service its meaning for him.[25]

Preaching and the Preacher

A further implication of our conception of preaching is a very personal one. If preaching is the re-enactment of the Deed of redemption in the lives of men, it is not likely to be consummated unless the preacher himself has been transformed by the Lord he proclaims and is a fit agent of the Redeemer. As the Captain of our salvation fulfilled his office not because of any ecclesiastical status, but by virtue of "the power of an endless life," so those who follow in his train as undershepherds must carry forward his mission by becoming personal agents of that same power. As Forsyth has put it, "The act of Grace can never be conveyed by men on whom it does not act." [26] There are exceptions, of course, but they serve merely to prove the rule, and they are not as numerous as is sometimes supposed. Many of the supposed exceptions are deceptive, because they are the result of secular measurements of success in the pulpit, and are

[25] *Memoirs of Childhood and Youth* (New York: The Macmillan Co., 1949), p. 45. Used by permission of The Macmillan Co.

[26] *Positive Preaching and the Modern Mind,* p. 79.

merely the product of the force of human personality or the clever tricks of the trade which may pack churches, keep an active program going, and gain a reputation for the minister as an outstanding representative of his calling, but do not do business with eternal things.

Really to preach, one must get men beyond himself to God. And it is true, whether we like to admit it or not, that often the richness of human gifts with which some preachers are endowed, which attract men to them personally, becomes a great liability in the real work of the kingdom. One of the most damaging judgments of a minister I ever heard was uttered inadvertently by a young admirer who was enthusiastically reporting on his wonderful sermon. Said he, "I became so interested in his cleverness of speech and his perfection of delivery that I forgot all about what he was saying!" What a compliment! As long as the minister and his words and gestures and cleverness are more central to the consciousness of the listener than is God, the whole affair is a human performance, producing nothing but "wood, hay, stubble," which cannot endure the burning fires of God's judgment. And although a rich endowment of human gifts can be used to the glory of God, the sinfulness of the human heart is such that it is the rare man who can use them humbly and selflessly and wholly to the glory of God.

The modern emphasis on pastoral work and the personal relationship between the minister and his people is, without doubt, a wholesome thing. But like every worthy gain, it has its dangers, which are all the more vicious just because they are so deeply hidden by outward success. Many a minister has mistaken a strong personal attachment to himself for an attachment to Jesus Christ. And many a man has mistaken an increased attendance resulting from a personal loyalty to him which makes his people go to church to avoid embarrassment when they see him or because they do not want to "let him down," for a movement of the Spirit of God. The results of this are to be seen in the fact that often when the preacher is gone, the people are gone, too. I have seen men sweep into a community and, by the force of personal dynamism, get people to attend church for a time who had not crossed the door of the church for fifteen years. But after that particular preacher left town, these same people did not darken the door of the church for the next fifteen years. The implications of this are obvious. One would not deny the fact, of course, that if people come to the house of worship out of sheer loyalty to the minister, the Spirit of God could speak to them and accomplish the Deed of redemption in spite of the false motivation under which they came. But what I am here pleading for is that we ministers do not allow ourselves to be deceived by gains which are the result of personal attachment to us rather than to God. "Was Paul crucified for you?" cried the Apostle (I Cor. 1:13). We must get men to believe in Christ, not in us.

One sometimes wonders whether, if our preaching were what it ought to be, we would need all the modern channels of personal contact which demand the presence of the minister at a score of meetings every week. Dr. Jowett said, in his maturity, that the minister who had had the most profound and lasting influence over his life and ministry was his boyhood pastor, Dr. Enoch Mellor, under whom he sat until he went off to school at the age of seventeen. And yet he never once met him personally! The family sat in the balcony and went out another door than the one where the minister greeted the people, and Jowett was never home as a boy on the few occasions when the minister called, so that he never once had the opportunity of shaking his

142

hand or speaking to him face to face. Yet this was the man who left his mark on him permanently, and who later became the pattern for his own great ministry.[27]

This instance may be, it is true, exceptional, but it raises the question whether, if preachers did what they should in preaching, the results, even if smaller, would not in the long run outweigh the more dramatic gains which spring from the level of mere human friendliness. Could it be that our efforts at keeping our churches going through the weight of personal contact is a subconscious confession that we fear that if people do not keep their loyalty to the church through their personal loyalty to us, they will not keep it? This may at least give us pause, if we are spiritually realistic enough to face it. I am in no sense decrying the value of the right sort of pastoral work, but I am pleading for an awareness that it must be properly geared into the work of preaching, and that unless it is, it may deceive us by human gains which shall "vanish like snow in the breath of the Lord" in the great day when the secrets of all hearts shall be revealed.

This means, then, that in true preaching the minister must strive to keep himself in the background to make room for Jesus Christ in the consciousness of those who hear him. James Denney's famous statement of fifty years ago is true for all time: "Young gentlemen, it is impossible to impress men with your own cleverness and at the same time to impress them with the wonder of Jesus Christ." And what is this but a paraphrase of Paul, who wrote to the Corinthians, "Plainly God's purpose was that your faith should rest not upon man's cleverness but upon the power of God" (I Cor. 2:5, Phillips)? We need to ponder this again and again until it "burns out the dross of base desire" and shatters our

[27] Arthur Porritt, *John Henry Jowett, C.H., M.A., D.D.* (New York: George H. Doran Co., 1924), pp. 12-15.

pride. We ministers have become too much a professional lot, trying to develop techniques and smooth tricks to make people think we are clever. Men don't get past us to God. They go away from our services saying, How fine is the preacher! But seldom do they go away saying, How great is my sin! or How great is the love of God! Said Paul, "If I speak with the tongues of men and of angels, . . . if I have . . . all knowledge; . . . if I have all faith, so as to remove mountains," I am *nothing* unless the agape, the life and love of God, dwells in me and is imparted through me (I Cor. 13:1-2, A.S.V.). And he wrote to the Corinthians, among whom human cleverness was valued greatly, that he had preached "not with eloquent wisdom, lest the cross of Christ be emptied of its power. . . . And I was with you in weakness and in much fear and trembling; and my speech and my message were not in plausible words of wisdom, but in demonstration of the Spirit and power, that your faith might not rest in the wisdom of men but in the power of God" (I Cor. 1:17, 2:3-5). Paul knew the dangers of influencing men by human cleverness rather than by the power of God, and he fought it like a dragon.

Let the preacher strive, then, to avoid all efforts to move men by anything but the power of the truth. Dr. Barrett, once president of the Congregational Union in England, gave a description of the preaching of Dean Church which enforces what we are here discussing: "I recall even now the spare figure, almost insignificant in its stature, standing in the pulpit, the upward look, then the quiet reading of the text, and then the whole vast congregation subdued into breathless attention, not by the spell of a great orator, but by the wonderful spiritual power of the man." [28] Spiritual

[28] D. C. Lathbury, *Dean Church* (London: A. R. Mowbray & Co., Ltd., 1912), p. 192.

power, not oratory! The power of the presence of Christ through his gospel, not the power of personal magnetism through human devices. We are not artists, actors, orators— we are preachers. And what may be a gain to other forms of speech may be a hindrance in preaching. As to speech, gesture, manner, it is well by thoughtful effort to train ourselves to avoid inelegancies which distract. But let us shrink as from a serpent from any attempt to develop skills that attract men to us. Decoration ill becomes the Cross. Elocution is blasphemy in the presence of the crucified. Anything which makes men marvel at us rather than at the redemption which we proclaim is cause not for glorying, but for penitence.

Francis of Assisi, it is said, was once applauded by his fellows at the conclusion of a sermon. He went home in tears to repent because men had applauded him rather than bowing in reverence at the feet of his Lord. Herein he was right. Let us not covet human applause, but let us with simplicity, without self-consciousness, avoiding all efforts to turn a clever phrase at which men will marvel, shunning artificial gestures, turning away from all tricks of psychology or mechanics designed to induce cheap emotion, proclaim the redemptive Deed of God in Christ until we have "placarded Christ crucified" before the eyes of men. If this does not move them, of what use is anything else? The greatest asset we can have in preaching is ourselves to believe the unbelievable good news we proclaim, and to live, through Christ, in the "power of an endless life." Sir Robertson Nicoll, in writing of the Scottish preaching of his boyhood, said, "Freshness, style, and the other qualities now held essential to popular sermons were unknown. But the preaching did its work, nevertheless, as George MacDonald says, because it *was preaching*—the rare speech of a man to his fellows, whereby they know that he is in his inmost heart a believer." [29]

Preaching and Redemption

A further implication of our definition of preaching is that all our preaching, to be Christian, must be definitely rooted in the broad context of redemption. Ethical preaching which is not directly related to the central fact of redemption is sub-Christian. Ethical behavior is but the outward expression of the soul's grasp of redemption. It reflects our understanding of the character of a redeeming God and our gratitude for the fact that even "while we were yet sinners Christ died for us" (Rom. 5:8). It is futile, therefore, to sever ethics from faith and to try to inculcate Christian patterns of behavior in the lives of people who know little or nothing of the character of God or of the incalculable cost of their redemption. The "Be good; please, be good" type of preaching which has little to say about the Incarnation, the Cross, the Resurrection, has been a major cause of Protestant ineffectiveness.

There is no more striking fact about the Bible, in both Old and New Testaments, than the constant linking of its appeal for ethical behavior with the great fact of redemption. The preaching of the prophets, whose passion for social righteousness has never been exceeded, always rooted the demand for righteousness and justice in loyalty to the covenant God who had redeemed them at the Exodus and sustained them ever afterward in continuing redemptive mercy. Micah, who has often been falsely used as a champion of "ethics without theology" because he wrote, "He hath showed thee, O man, what is good; and what doth Jehovah

[29] T. H. Darlow, *William Robertson Nicoll, Life and Letters* (London: Hodder & Stoughton, 1925), p. 6.

require of thee, but to do justly, and to love kindness, and to walk humbly with thy God?" (Micah 6:8, A.S.V.) prefaced these classic words just a few verses before with this: "O my people, what have I done unto thee? and wherein have I wearied thee? testify against me. For I brought thee up out of the land of Egypt, and redeemed thee out of the house of bondage; . . . remember from Shittim unto Gilgal, that ye may know *the righteous acts of Jehovah*" (Micah 6:3-5, A.S.V.; italics mine). In his hatred of religion without ethics, Micah did not plead for ethics without theology. Rather, he saw clearly that ethical behavior was lacking because his people had forgotten the mighty redemptive deeds of their God, and he called for a deepening of their awareness of *God's righteous acts* as the only valid stimulus to righteous acts on their own part. Amos' demand that "justice roll down as waters, and righteousness as a mighty stream" (5:24, A.S.V.), and his devastating rebukes to those who "sold the righteous for silver, and the needy for a pair of shoes" (2:6, A.S.V.), were directly rooted in this: "I brought you up out of the land of Egypt, and led you forty years in the wilderness. . . . You only have I known of all the families of the earth" (2:10; 3:2, A.S.V.). In relating ethics to the Deed of redemption, these prophets were simply expressing that which is to be found at the very heart of the Old Testament from beginning to end.

The New Testament is no less explicit in this matter. Paul sought to foster unity among the Philippian Christians not by telling them that everyone would be better off if they loved one another, but by turning their minds to the incarnation, the cross, and the resurrection of Jesus (Phil. 2:5 ff.). In like manner, he incited the Corinthians to moral behavior by reminding them, "You are not your own; for you were bought with a price" (I Cor. 6:19-20). Peter, in a plea for faithfulness in suffering, set forth the motivation, "For Christ also died for sins once for all, the righteous for the unrighteous, that he might bring us to God" (I Pet. 3:18). And in counseling sobriety of life, he bases his appeal first on the character of God—"You shall be holy, for I am holy" (I Pet. 1:16); then on the Deed of redemption—"You know that you were ransomed from the futile ways inherited from your fathers, not with perishable things such as silver or gold, but with the precious blood of Christ, like that of a lamb without blemish or spot" (I Pet. 1:18-19).

These are but a few examples, which could be multiplied indefinitely, of the fact that in the Bible ethical demands are always the outgrowth of redemptive deeds. The structure of the prophetic writings and of the Gospels and Epistles consistently suggests that the facts of redemption were the set of data upon which all biblical thinking proceeded. And in this respect the biblical writers were true to their Lord. C. H. Dodd writes:

Whether we say that the apostolic preaching was modelled on that of Jesus, or that the evangelist formulated his summary of the preaching of Jesus on the model of that of the primitive Church, at any rate the two are identical in purport. The Kingdom of God is conceived as coming in the events of the life, death, and resurrection of Jesus, and to proclaim these facts, in their proper setting, is to preach the Gospel of the Kingdom of God.[30]

And any preaching not thus rooted can lay no claim to being Christian.

It is possible, even, to preach Christ in a sub-Christian way, if our preaching of him is preoccupied with facets of his human personality and items of his ethical teaching divorced from their profound relation to his redemptive death

[30] *Op. cit.*, p. 24.

and resurrection. Much preaching of the Sermon on the Mount in Christian pulpits is sub-Christian, for the counsels there offered are frequently torn from their context in the Gospels and set forth unrelated to the total work of the One who gave them. The Sermon on the Mount was preserved only by men who placed it in a book, the major attention of which is given to the events which cluster around the close of Jesus' life; and as Cullmann has recently pointed out, the meaning of the Sermon on the Mount can be understood in Christian terms only as one sees it as the ethical expression of faith in the redemptive deeds of Jesus.[31]

It is not to be insisted on, of course, that to be Christian every sermon must explicitly mention the redemptive deeds. If this were so, there would be little time left for anything else in the pulpit. But for preaching to be truly Christian, however narrow or specific the truth that is enforced in any one sermon, both preacher and people must set this specific truth in the broad context of redemption and view it from the standpoint which would have prevailed if its relation to the Deed of redemption were set forth. On this, Principal Rainy many years ago spoke an effective word:

It is one of the good features of the modern time, that the central place in Christianity of our Lord's person, His wondrous self, has become more generally recognized. Hence preaching revolves more constantly on this centre: and studies in the life of Christ form a more predominant and characteristic feature of our preaching, surely with advantage. And yet here, also, one is struck sometimes by a mere parsimonious insistence on the immediate incident or feature in hand, illustrated and presented only as a phase of human goodness worthy of attention and admiration. On this point I will not be peremptory in my censure. For I suppose this may be so done that the sense of who and what

[31] *The Earliest Christian Confessions,* tr. J. K. S. Reid (London: The Lutterworth Press, 1949), p. 12.

He is, whose goodness is in hand, may arise in the mind all the more inevitably because little is said of it. . . . But yet I must say that, as a rule, to preach on a portion of the life of Christ precisely as a modern Socinian might, is not like to perform the office which the history was meant to serve.

In a word, there is a kingdom of heaven, an economy of salvation, existing and revealed. It is not to be the matter of every sermon to enumerate its elements, and detail the relations of them. It may well be the matter of many sermons to make a minute study and application of matters that are in the nature of details, single principles, or aspects of things. In doing that, the topic is to be dealt with as it is, according to its own nature and conditions, not denaturalised and twisted to accommodate it to more remote interest. Yet it ought to be treated so that preacher and hearers feel themselves on the ground of the kingdom of heaven, and have it as part of their business to see how the topic in hand takes its place in that great system.[32]

Carnegie Simpson, the biographer of Principal Rainy, reinforced this word of Rainy's by a comparison of the preaching of two of Scotland's great ministers, Chalmers and Blair. Chalmers was "the great evangelical moralist of the Scottish pulpit," whose ethical preaching breathed the atmosphere of redemption and has left a permanent mark on Scottish life and character. Blair, on the other hand, was a "typical moderate moralist," whose "elegant eloquence" won him much praise in his day, but whose preaching made little permanent contribution to Scottish life and whose sermons are now as "flat as decanted champagne." [33]

Preaching and the Cross

A final consideration which follows from our definition of preaching is that if preaching is to re-enact redemption,

[32] P. Carnegie Simpson, *The Life of Principal Rainy* (London: Hodder & Stoughton, 1909), I, 418-19. Used by permission.
[33] *Ibid.*, p. 419. Used by permission.

it must have the tragic note of redemption in it. The times in which we live have brought into sharp focus the element of tragedy in human experience. A religion with a less tragic note than that of the human heartbreak to which it seeks to minister will be thrust aside in life's crises as an impediment that can well be got rid of. The lag which has overtaken the church in other parts of the world has not yet struck us in America, for tragedy has not yet struck us on the scale that it has elsewhere. But it is probably coming. And when it comes, the easy, comfortable religion which now passes for Christianity with many of us will not suffice. Our fussy, human religiousness which keeps church programs going and sends us through the motions of religion will not hold us steady when everything is shaken that can be shaken. We must move among the abiding certainties of the "kingdom that cannot be shaken" if we are to have any word of light or power for men when they go down into the abyss. Thirty years ago, Harris E. Kirk warned us that the church needs to be "relocated . . . in the eternal order of things." [34] This is even more true today. Why should a tragic world turn to us for a word picked up in the temporalities? We have glamorized Christmas and Easter into sentimental and beautiful nothingness; we have coated over the bitter realities of life and death with a veneer of pious sentiment which will not stand up under the test of the soul's last wretchedness when the cry is forced from anguished lips, "My God, my God, why?" We have become so much like the world that we have no unique word of life to offer it. And as someone has pointed out, in becoming so much like the world, we have become distant from it; for if we have nothing to say to men but the things with

[34] *Op. cit.,* p. 181.

which they are already familiar, why should they not pass us by and let us alone?

Ibsen, in his *Brand*, characterized the loss of tragic depth in our Christianity:

> Salvation had been cheaplier priced
> Had *your* God ruled: the Crucified
> For mercy from the cross had cried,
> And our redemption had been given
> By diplomatic note from heaven! [35]

Through this loss of the note of tragedy in our message, we have sold our birthright for a miserable mess of trivialities. The Cross is the point at which tragedy is brought to a focus as nowhere else. There, through pain, desolation, and nameless agony, suffering Love was stabbed and slain, until there is no man who ever lived who cannot hear in the cry "My God, my God, why hast thou forsaken me?" the echo of a deeper bitterness than he has known. And on Easter the final contradiction was resolved. In a way we can never understand and little imagine, suffering Love set the cosmic tragedy right and conquered forever all that issues in death. So that every man, with the universe crumbling at his feet, can cry out in his heart, "Hallelujah! For the Lord our God the Almighty reigns" (Rev. 19:6).

The Cross and the Resurrection are ours to preach! With them as the center of our preaching we may have to await more tragic days for a hearing. But what of that, if when men finally turn to us, we have something to say that will heal the soul's last wretchedness? The tragic note of redemption is the foundation on which all our preaching must

[35] Everyman's Library edition (New York: E. P. Dutton & Co., 1915), p. 98. Used by permission.

be based. And we will recover the power of the pulpit when we discover that sermons are what Charles E. Jefferson once characterized them, "drops of blood shed by the servants of the Lord for the redemption of the world." [36]

[36] *The Minister as Prophet* (New York: Thomas Y. Crowell & Co., 1905), p. 60.

Index of Scripture References

OLD TESTAMENT

NEW TESTAMENT

Index of Subjects

Aestheticism, 119-20
Ainsworth, Percy, 16, 100
Altar, 124, 126
Amos, 81, 104
Angels, 138
Apostles, the preaching of the, 23-24, 30-32
Aquinas, Thomas, 40
Archimedes, 98
Augustine, 40
Authority, of the Bible, 69-72; in preaching, 111-12

Baptism, 124, 126
Bacon, Francis, 83
Balance of truth, 82, 91-98
Barrett, George S., 144
Barth, Karl, 130
Beecher, Henry Ward, 103, 106-7, 109
Bible, the, and abiding realities, 98-102; authoritative in religion only, 72-73; authority of, 55-61, 64-65; catholicity of, 96; and Christian unity, 64-65; its conception of God, 20; its conception of itself, 67-69; contemporary illiteracy of, 104-5; corrective for false success, 115-18; corrective for overemphases, 95-98; corrective for pseudo Christianity, 107-8; in the early church, 52-53; and ecumenicity, 63-64; function of, 65-69; as "good news," 68; and the gos-

Bible—cont'd
pel, 59; as historic record, 69; and the Holy Spirit, 59-60; human element of, 69-75; inexhaustible riches of, 88-91; inspiration of, 66, 79-80; as instrument, 65-69; and the minister's soul, 80-81; nature of, 67-68; nature of its authority, 69-72; neglect of in preaching, 37-39; normative for preaching, 53-54; and pastoral ministry, 83-85; as preacher's charter, 41-42; preacher's guardian in controversy, 102-3; the preacher's preacher, 80-81; problem of interpretation, 73-80; and Protestantism, 57; record of God's acts, 20-22, 41; as redemptive deed, 55-57; "rediscovery" of, 7, 62; relation to Jesus, 68; sometimes misleading, 74; sourcebook for sermons, 87-91; and theology, 81-83; and tradition, 57-61; uniqueness of, 39-41; use by early apologists, 52-53;
Blair, Hugh, 150
Body of Christ, the, 96, 111, 128, 130, 132, 135, 139
Brand, 152
Brastow, Lewis O., 102
Brooks, Phillips, 18
Burns, Robert, 94
Bushnell, Horace, 134

157

Date Due